William Thompson

(1775–1833)

WILLIAM THOMPSON

(1775–1833)

Pioneer Socialist

RICHARD K. P. PANKHURST

PLUTO PRESS
London ● Concord, Mass

This edition first published 1991 by Pluto Press
345 Archway Road, London N6 5AA
and 141 Old Bedford Road,
Concord, MA 01742, USA

First published in 1954

British Library Cataloguing in Publication Data
Pankhurst, Richard
  William Thompson 1775–1833.
  1. Ireland. Socialism. Thompson, William 1775–1833
  I. Title
  335.0092

  ISBN 0–7453–0517–2 hb

Library of Congress Cataloging in Publication Data
Pankhurst, Richard Keir Pethick, 1927–
    William Thompson (1775–1833) : pioneer socialist / Richard K.P.
  Pankhurst.
      p.   cm.
    Reprint. Originally published : London : Watts, 1954.
    Includes bibliographical references.
    ISBN 0–7453–0517–2 hb
    1. Thompson, William, 1775–1833.   2. Socialists—Great Britain–
  –Biography.   I. Title.
  HX244.7.T46P36   1991
  335′.0092—dc20
  [B]   90–6874
                                                             CIP

Typeset by BP Integraphics Ltd, Bath
Printed in Great Britain by Billing and Sons Ltd, Worcester

Contents

Foreword

H. L. BEALES

William Thompson described himself on the title page of his *Labour Rewarded* (1827) as 'one of the idle classes'. Idle, as we all know, is a difficult term. A candid working engineer once told me that he had never worked 'all out' in his day-to-day employment but always toiled with real fury in his garden: as one would guess, he was a socialist – i.e. an individualist. Samuel Smiles filled his capitalist pantheon with socialistically-minded and individualistic entrepreneurs who strained themselves most intensely when they had obtained their major objectives of wealth and economic power so that they might leave their world better than they found it. William Thompson, though not, as he said, what is usually called a labourer, composed three major works of deep social analysis in five years. Already for a decade at the opening of this fruitful period he had been living on what he called 'rent, the produce of the labour of others' (a definition that was in itself rather shocking!), and so he set himself the task of finding out how Labour might acquire the whole product of its labour, and the claims of Capital and Labour might be 'conciliated' – to the destruction of himself and all other rentiers. ... But the only sanity, we are discovering, is in paradox, and the multiplication of paradoxical institutions and behaviours is of the essence of liberty, equality, and fraternity. So William Thompson is our contemporary, a living old master, who deserves the recognition that is so grudgingly given to open-minded sectarians in our sect-ridden world.

A substantial study of William Thompson has long been overdue. Socialists talk at least as much as feminists, free-thinkers, and co-operators, but though Thompson pioneers in all their fields, neither singly nor in collaboration (!) have they produced a life of him. This neglect is now ended by Dr Richard Pankhurst. Coming as he does of crusading stock, he tackled his subject with great zest. Even the embarrassing elusiveness of Thompson's life did not daunt him, and I much admired as his work progressed, the skill with which he made a nest out of unlikely straws in contrary winds and the tenacity with which he refused to get tired even though most of the roads to success proved to be mere blind alleys. I would like to add that it was Harold Laski who first suggested the subject to him, which is one more proof of that great teacher's capacity to set venturesome researchers to work at appropriate tasks.

The English democratic pantheon is not very well furnished. The only published life of Thomas Hodgskin is still that of Halévy, which was issued just fifty years ago and is still untranslated; someday, perhaps, Cecil Driver of Yale will put us in his debt for that MS. on Hodgskin still in his study drawer, as he did for his brilliant life of Richard Oastler. It may be that this life of Thompson will provide the encouragement. Charles Hall, John Minter Morgan, Hetherington, even Major Cartwright (whose grave crumbles in squalid neglect in a suburban churchyard in Finchley a hundred yards from where I am now writing), and a host of others are still waiting for their biographers. Even worse is the increasing pile of good unpublished studies – Dr A. Schoyen's brilliant *George Julian Harney*, Dr Plummer's *Bronterre O'Brien*, Mr Graham's *Joseph Hume*, Yahoda's study of *J. M. Robertson*, (whose centenary falls next year), and a host of others. ... Do we really deserve our democrats?

Preface

This work is based on a successful doctoral thesis presented at the London School of Economics and Political Science. The subject was suggested by the late Professor H. J. Laski, under whom I was privileged to study and from whom I received to the full that kind help and encouragement for which he was justly renowned.

I wish to express my grateful thanks to Mr H. L. Beales, Reader in Economic History at the London School of Economics, for his constant interest and advice throughout the progress of this work; his wide knowledge of the nineteenth-century literature it was necessary to consult was of inestimable value.

I would also acknowledge my debt to other members of the academic staff of the London School of Economics, notably to Mr W. Pickles, who put me on the track of material relating to Mrs Wheeler, to Mr W. H. Morris-Jones, and to Dr H. S. Reiss, who assisted me in obtaining important material in Ireland. Grateful thanks are also due to Mr P. Sraffa, Director of Research at Trinity College, Cambridge, who gave me access to a then unpublished letter in the Bentham-Ricardo correspondence; to Mr John Wilks, the Librarian of University College, London, who placed the Bentham manuscripts at my disposal; and to Miss Digby of the Co-operative Reference Library, Mr A. R. Perkins of the Co-operative Productive Federation, Mr D. Flanagan of the Library of the Co-operative Union, and Mr R. L. Marshall and his staff at the Co-operative College, all of whom greatly facilitated my study of the literature now in the possession of the Co-operative Movement. I received help and encouragement also from Professor G. D. H. Cole and from Dr W. Stark, Lecturer in Social Studies at the University of Edinburgh, from the late Lord Hamilton of Dalzell, and from Lady Emily Lutyens. Mr Michael Sadleir and Mrs Dora Neill Raymond most kindly assisted my research into feminist ideas; and Messrs Longmans Green went to great trouble in quest of information concerning the circulation of Thompson's books.

ix

It would be impossible in this Preface to acknowledge the many debts incurred to the numerous correspondents who replied to my letters in the Press. Special reference, however, must be made to the help received from H.E. the High Commissioner for Ireland; the Deputy Keeper of the Irish Public Record Office; Mr A. MacLocklain, Irish Chief Herald and Genealogical Officer; the Director of the National Library of Ireland; Mr Sean MacCarthy, the Lord Mayor of Cork; Mr Eugene Carberry, Cork City Librarian; Professor Busteed of Cork University College; Mr Sean O'Coinealain, President of the Cork Historical Society; Mr F. J. P. Burgoyn, Librarian of the Belfast Linen Hall Library, and the Venerable R. Beresford Poer, Dean of Ross.

During my visit to William Thompson's birthplace in West Cork Fathers Kelly, O'Callaghan, and Bourke generously gave me every aid and introduced me to local residents, among whom I must specially thank Nurse O'Callaghan, Mrs O'Donovan, and Mr Jim Daley of Connonagh, for sharing with me interesting local traditions concerning William Thompson. I am indebted also to many other citizens of County Cork, among them Mr G. F. Brewitt of Messrs F. H. Thompson and Son Ltd, and to the editor of the *Cork Examiner*, Mr Emmet O'Donovan of Union Hall, and to Mr W. J. Kingston, Mr D. P. McCarthy, and Mrs Wolfe of Skibbereen. In Dublin Mr Patrick Lynch and Mr Desmond Ryan were both of unfailing assistance.

Professor Arthur E. Bestor, Jr., of the University of Illinois, Professor Joseph Dorfman of the University of Columbia, Professor Bernard Drell of the University of Chicago, Mr Burton W. Atkinson, the Director of the Reference Department of the Library of Congress, and the late Agnes Inglis of the Labadie Collection of the University of Michigan, all gave me great help in locating early Socialist literature in the United States.

Woodford Green,   R. K. P. P.
Essex
January 1954

1

Background and Early Life

William Thompson was the most important theoretician among the early Socialists. He was one of the two outstanding leaders in the Co-operative Movement in these islands, from which the Socialist ideal had its birth. He anticipated Marx in many of his theories, and even coined some of the definitions and terminology of politico-economic phenomena which the 'founder of scientific Socialism' subsequently employed.

Engels himself declared that the early English Socialist literature was 'more ample' than its counterpart on the Continent, had 'done wonders for the education of the proletariat,' and 'could not be surpassed' until the appearance of Marx's *Capital*.

Professor Laski stated that the writings of Thompson and his colleagues were 'really superb,' and that no one could read them without a sense that 'their case against capitalism must be answered, and that it was not easy to answer.'[1]

Not only were the writings of William Thompson pre-eminent in the sphere of early Socialism and Co-operation, he was also a pioneer in the cause of the emancipation of women. No book published before his time on this subject, even the famous work of Mary Wollstonecraft, is at once so broad and comprehensive and so direct and practical as Thompson's *Appeal of One Half the Human Race*.

Nevertheless, though his works were widely known and discussed in his time and greatly influenced the Co-operative, Trade Unionist, and Chartist movements, they were rigidly ignored by the orthodox economists and regarded with intense disfavour in conventional circles. In the 120 odd years since his death he has gradually ceased to be known in this country, except to a restricted circle of the more erudite students of political and economic theory, though the value of his work has been more fully recognized by Continental authors.

Despite the immense value of his pioneer work on the most important social problems of his time, his books have long been out of print;

1

no biography has been written. The present essay has been undertaken to remedy this neglect as well as to introduce to the public of today the ideas of a pioneer student and thinker whose contributions to social theory are still apposite and controversial and still vividly illuminate many a social problem of our own day.

William Thompson was born at Cork in 1775. His ancestors were some of those 'adventurous' Englishmen who acquired land in Ireland between 1682 and 1686. His family belonged to the Protestant 'ascendancy' which held the monopoly of all State positions – all power and patronage and most of the wealth and education in the land. By birth and marriage they were well-to-do landed proprietors scattered throughout County Cork; most of them were members of the Established Church of Ireland, though a few became followers of John Wesley. There is little trace of any reforming spirit among them; with few exceptions they belonged to the class of absentee landlords who, as a member of the family admitted, 'discouraged every kind of improvement by denying leases to their tenants.'

William was the grandson of a Protestant divine and the son of Alderman John Thompson, one of the richest merchants of Cork, who served at various times as Speaker and Mayor of the Municipality, and as High Sheriff of the County, being subsequently appointed Freeman-at-large. At his death in 1814 he left his family in very easy circumstances. William took over the Cork family business with its little fleet of trading vessels, and became the owner of an estate of some 1,400 acres of rocky land overlooking the lovely little harbour of Glandore, some forty miles away.

Cork, in those days, was renowned as the second city of Ireland, a prosperous commercial centre supplying beef, butter, and other local produce to the merchant ships which plied between Britain and North America. But behind the paper facade of prosperity the masses lived in a poverty and squalor which beggared description; one English traveller recorded that the poor quarter was 'a moving mass of rags and dirt, swearing, obscenity and fighting.' The city, however, was well supplied with libraries and learned societies, and was frequently visited by lecturers of international repute. Thompson himself was one of the proprietors of the Cork Institution and a prominent member of the local Philosophical, Scientific, and Literary Society. His residence, one of the lofty houses, faced with blue slate, in fine, open St Patrick Street, the elegant quarter of the town, contained an extensive library.

His formative years were lived in a period when the ancient ways of life were being shattered by the twin forces of the French and Industrial Revolutions. The old order was collapsing or disintegrating under violent social upheavals. All over Europe, and in the young American Republic, adventurous thinkers were questioning the very bases of traditional society and laying the foundations of new social thought. Like many thinkers of his time, Thompson held a passionate belief in the possibility of discovering a 'social science' which, by revealing the working of social forces, would lead to the eradication of social ills and inaugurate an era of universal happiness and well-being. He long avoided becoming a partisan of any one school, hoping that the theories propounded by the economists, the rationalists, and such moral philosophers as Godwin and Bentham might be fused together for the benefit of the human race. In pursuit of this ideal he read widely, entered into personal relations with many of the social pioneers of his day, and visited the experiments conducted under their auspices.

He travelled a good deal and spent some time in France and the Low Countries. It was probably on one of these journeys that he established contacts with the Saint-Simonians, whose theories he examined with interest. He studied also the works of Sismondi and others of the 'modern school' of French political economists who considered, as he says, that the 'tendency of civilization and of manufacturing improvements was to deteriorate the situation of the industrious classes as compared with that of the idle classes.' These Continental associations caused Irish provincialism to dub him a 'Red Republican' – it was even declared that he went about poverty-stricken Glandore with a French tricolour 'at the end of his walking-stick.'

The vivid contrast between the 'two nations' and the callous class pride of the wealthy section of Cork society, from which he sprang, drove him into bitterly intransigent opposition to the social attitudes of his family circle. In the elections of 1812 and 1826 he gave his support to Christopher Hely-Hutchinson, whose advocacy of Catholic Emancipation had incurred the hatred of Thompson's own Protestant kith and kin. He denounced the capitalist system, complaining that 'those who labour are overcome with toil, while the idle classes who live on the products of the labourer are almost equally wretched from lack of occupation.' He declared that under a just system moderate exertions would be made obligatory to all, the 'two master-evils of society,' excessive toil and excessive idleness, being thus avoided.

When in 1814, at the age of thirty-nine, he took over his estate at Glandore he was confronted by all the problems of the Irish land question: the poverty and squalor of the tenants, their primitive agricultural methods, the ruthless exactions of middlemen who exploited them in the interests of parasitic absentee landlords, and the continuous evictions which had driven huge sections of the ragged, semi-starving population to the verge of rebellion. He immediately determined to break with the established custom of absentee landlordship. He spent much of his time on his estate, gave leases on generous terms to his tenants, and instituted improved methods of cultivation.

In accordance with the latest agricultural theories, a suitable portion of his own farm was placed under spade cultivation and dug over to the depth of two spades. As a practical example to his tenantry he laid out a model cottage farm of five acres, comprising a one-acre garden, fenced and stocked with fruit-trees and root crops, and a further four acres devoted to the scientific rotation of crops. On it he built a cottage with cowhouse, dairy, beehives, and pigsty, and gave possession to a peasant of good character with full power to consume and enjoy all he could produce, but 'strictly bound him to cultivate every patch of it by spade in the manner he had prescribed as most exemplary.' To further the improvement of agriculture he also erected a school, where the children of his tenants were taught spade cultivation 'on the latest plan' and were given 'all the produce they could grow.'

Conscious of the need for secondary industries, which were at that time virtually non-existent in Ireland, he investigated the possibilities of producing silk and linen, and laid plans for establishing a deep-sea fishery near Glandore. He set about the widening of the Rowrey River, which linked his estate with that port.

His efforts for social amelioration are mentioned in the 1834 report of the House of Commons Select Committee inquiring into drunkenness. They are described in the evidence of John Finch, a Liverpool merchant and leading advocate of Co-operation, who visited Glandore in 1833, presumably on a visit to Thompson. Finch told the Committee that 800 acres of the estate had formerly been 'crowded' by some 700 beggars on the verge of starvation; under enlightened management, however, it had been broken up into allotments of from three to twenty acres, depending on the size of the tenant's family, and made available on a three-year trial period, after which long leases had been signed by mutual agreement if the tenants had proved amenable to methods of improved cultivation. Each allotment was provided with a neat slate-roofed cottage; ploughs, harrows, articles of household furniture, and other requirements were lent to the tenants, and could be purchased by annual instalments. Out of sixty families, fifty-seven had 'paid their rent every farthing'; the remaining three had only failed 'in consequence of some family misfortune.' The numerous dram-shops which formerly existed had all been closed, except two which were 'placed in a conspicuous part of the village' accessible only from the main street; anyone wishing to enter being obliged to do so in the public view. The deterrent effect was such that even the two remaining shops were deserted. 'The whole place had become sober and industrious; all were doing well. Ignorance, poverty, drunkenness, and crime had been banished.' The village magistrate had reported that 'scarcely a case of crime came before him in a year': the Government had in consequence suspended the office.

Thompson constantly kept under review the innovations introduced by progressive agriculturalists, and himself made many experiments. He noticed that Charles Whitlaw had discovered a better way of cooking potatoes, and eagerly commented that this should be valuable to potato-eating Ireland. He was delighted when one of his friends, Joseph Johnson, a working chemist of Youghal, invented a new method of extracting sugar from the potato. He predicted a promising future for the new root crops, beet and mangel-wurzel, and distributed seeds to local farmers to give them the opportunity of cultivating them.

His kindness and his eccentricities were for many years into the present century the subject of talk among the old folk of Glandore and Rosscarbery, who learnt of him from their parents or grandparents as their friend and protector, the best of all landlords and employers. His personal frugality and moderation caused general astonishment; for the most part, men of his class then ate and drank heavily and the poor were perforce denied their appetites. For the last seventeen years of his life he was a non-smoker, vegetarian, and teetotaller, declaring he could thus read and write better. His breakfast would be bread and jam; he would lunch on potatoes and turnips, refusing all suggestion of eggs or butter. His drink would be tea, sweetened with honey, a beverage abundantly supplied at all times to his workpeople. Honey was produced in great quantities on his farm, and his fondness for it became legendary. It is said that when inspecting his hives he once found a mouse in one of them which had become imprisoned by a coating of the sweet food it had come to steal. He seized it and licked it clean before releasing it to scamper away – a characteristic act of understanding tenderness for the helpless and the weak.

His experiments in novel feeding-stuffs gave rise to many rumours, sometimes growing into fantastic legends. It is told that having read that the flesh and bones of living animals contain ingredients similar to the components of wood, he purchased a number of young pigs and fed them on sawdust, peat, and straw, whereat, the diet failing to satisfy their pangs of hunger, the porkers maintained a chorus of lively squeals.

Popularly known as 'the philosopher,' he was regarded as a magician by some of the local folk. He was in fact an ardent student of chemistry and of other then rapidly expanding sciences on which he attended many lectures, including a course by the famous Sir Humphry Davy. Thompson himself delivered a number of public lectures and gave demonstrations for the edification of his neighbours.

It is said in the locality that he read the latest books on medicine, tested their theories on his sick neighbours, and when he effected a cure he would jokingly tell his patients not to thank God but his pills and the devil. Such atheistic utterances were regarded indulgently by an unquestioning Catholic community because of his unfailing kindness and good humour. He was at all times impatient of conventions, and vigorously denounced the acceptance without inquiry of traditional practices. He expressed blunt contempt for many professed remedies, since wholly discarded, prescribed by the medical men of his time. He also vigorously assailed the exactions of lawyers and the then interminable and costly processes of the law. Priests, doctors, and lawyers were in fact the ceaseless target of his denunciations.

Despite all the changes and trials of more than a century, memories of the Glandore Socialist have been handed down with affectionate reverence in the neighbourhood, and his plans for the prosperity of the area are still discussed with enthusiasm. His justice to his workpeople and his insistence that all should be equal and none oppressed are still extolled. Yet, despite his kindness, he had a passion for efficiency, castigated idleness, and insisted upon conscientious work from everyone. He protested bitterly against the excessive numbers of Church holidays which took the peasants away from essential work on their farms with their meagre yields and appalling poverty. Local villagers still chuckle over some of his sayings, such as his description of St Peter and St Paul as 'two of the greatest vagabonds,' uttered when chiding a couple of labourers who had absented themselves from work on the excuse that they had been celebrating the festival of those saints.

His constant efforts to improve the lot of his tenants notwithstanding, he was at times depressed by a sense of guilt at being a landlord deriving his income from the toil of poverty-stricken peasants and labourers; for he was profoundly convinced that human labour was the source of all wealth. He expressed what he regarded as the contradiction in his own life when he writes:

I am not what is usually called a labourer. Under equitable social arrangements, possessed of health and strength, I ought to blush in making this declaration. For the last twelve years of my life I have been living on what is called rent, the produce of the labour of others.[2]

In contemplating the inequality of the social system and his own privileged position, he determined to acquire personal redemption by devoting himself to the welfare of others. He hoped thereby, as he said, to 'raise' himself 'to an equality of usefulness with the productive classes.'

His first incursion into public affairs took place in 1818 when he appeared as a champion of popular education and pedagogical reform. As a proprietor of the Cork Institution he was appalled to discover its Government endowment entirely misused. Having made all the protests possible at meetings of the proprietors, he addressed his complaints to the public at large through a series of letters to the *Cork Southern Reporter*; these he subsequently published in pamphlet form under the title, *Practical Education for the South of Ireland*. He claimed that the Cork Institution had been founded to provide a liberal education at low cost for the children of the middle class 'to whom the possibility of anything more than a school education of writing and arithmetic and enough of Latin to be useless' had hitherto been denied. He argued that a person earning two or three hundred pounds a year – a substantial income for the middle class at that time – found it impossible to educate his children when boarding-schools charged from £40 to £100 per annum. Even 'gentlemen and merchants' with £1,000 a year were 'distressed' by the education of a large family. The period when the adolescent was too old for school and too young for business could be devoted to education, but this must be provided for not more than £10 per child.

The Cork Institution would have been 'admirably calculated' to fulfil this need had it not been 'most unwisely managed' so as to degenerate into 'a little sphere of private intrigue and favouritism.' Only £300 a year was applied to the payment of lecturers, in violation of the Charter, which stated that £900 must be so expended. An annual subsidy to agriculture of £900 was not publicly advertised but mysteriously disposed of by 'secret upstairs committee management'; another £200 was wasted yearly on a superintendent of a Natural History Museum who lacked ability to explain the specimens under his charge: 'a very sober and decent gentleman' employed purely 'for taking the trouble of going to bed, rising at a genteel hour, ornamenting the elegant room of the Institution-house, and perhaps reading therein during the day.' In the absence of any public instruction, the 'moths, stones, and Indian arrows' he guarded were 'so much useless lumber.' The library, upon which £300 a year was lavished, was denied to the public, being reserved for the exclusive use of the thirty or forty proprietors, who scarcely ever used it. A spectacular contrast was afforded by the Cork Public Library, which met the requirements of 400 families at much less expense and imposed no charge on the public purse. The Institution's lectures on agriculture were 'almost unattended,' the Irish agriculturalist not being interested in the 'sandy turnip and barley soil of Norfolk.'

It is evident that what Thompson desired was an institute which would provide an education nearly equivalent to that of a modern secondary school, but which would also devote attention to the social sciences and the ethics of citizenship; the curriculum he envisaged included the philosophy of history, the 'progress of human society,' outlines of the British Constitution, political economy, morals and ethics, literature, natural history, natural philosophy, chemistry, and agriculture.

Almost everyone could be trained to derive pleasure from 'general literature, from a cultivated taste and acquaintance with the poets and prose writers of his native tongue, and from dead and foreign writers by means of translations.'

The Institution should aim:

> not to make linguists, or mathematicians, or astronomers, or antiquarian dilettanti, but to make useful citizens for active life, to make intelligent and respectable, and benevolent tradesmen and merchants and country gentlemen, and to make their wives and daughters equally intelligent, respectable and useful.

In Thompson's rationalist *schema* there was no place for early nineteenth-century theology, which brooked no accommodation with science of any kind. He applied a Benthamite criticism to the educational system, which he declared should have 'utility' for its 'polar star.' He ridiculed the time spent on the study of the dead languages and stigmatized as absurd the fact that in a commercial city:

all the efforts of education should be directed, and almost confined, to the acquisition of a dead or even living language, to the learning how to express, by two or three combinations of letters, those scanty ideas of folly by the expression of which any one language, any one combination of letters would be disgraced.

The study of the classics, he ironically declared, was 'never made available to any useful purpose'; 'not a word of information' was given concerning 'the history, principles, processes, and effects of manufactures and commerce.'

With characteristic exuberance of phrase and a florid diction unusual even in his day, he described the sottish behaviour, too common at the time, whereby evenings were dissipated in 'stupid, disease-engendering gluttony and drinking,' the ladies 'savagely driven from the table, that men may, without blushing, turn themselves into brutes.' Education could cure the sensuality and tediousness of existence; it would ensure the 'polished decencies of social life.' University life did not escape this castigation: its 'ruinous habits of gambling' and its 'intemperance and sensuality' 'corroded the heart and the intellect, undermined the stoutest constitution, and either hurled to an inglorious grave or sowed thickly the seeds of disorders that tormented life for ten or twenty years, and then terminated a useless and froward existence' – an observation supported by numerous memoirs of the period.

2

Early Days with Bentham and Owen

William Thompson was deeply interested in Jeremy Bentham's new doctrine of Utilitarianism, and when engaged upon his *Practical Education* he made a careful study of Bentham's writings on education and submitted to him a questionnaire regarding the use of models for demonstration purposes, the best ways of simplifying teaching, and the means by which mere memorizing could be replaced by real understanding. He questioned Bentham's proposals in so far as they appeared to destroy the continuity of studies in the various subjects of the curriculum.[1]

The philosopher replied, on April 7, 1819, with a critical account of the teaching establishments he had inspected. Differing from Thompson on this point, he argued that memorizing could be used as a basis for subsequent understanding.

> You must either lose a great many years of time [he asserted] or be content with a very weak association between the signs and the ideas. But once the signs are lodged in the memory, and the corresponding ideas, by ever so weak a string, hooked on to them, the association becomes gradually stronger and stronger, and the ideas clearer and more expanded.[2]

This correspondence on a subject in which both were profoundly interested resulted in an invitation from the Utilitarian philosopher dated September 29, 1819, and couched in the following terms:

> During your stay in London, my hermitage, such as it is, is at your service, and you will be expected in it. I am a single man, turned seventy; but as far from melancholy as a man need be. Hour of dinner, six; tea, between nine and ten; bed, a quarter before eleven; dinner and tea in society; breakfast, my guests, whoever they are,

have at their own hour and by themselves: my breakfast, of which a newspaper, read to me to save my weak eyes, forms an indispensable part, I take by myself. Wine, I drink none, being, in that particular, of the persuasion of Jonadab, the son of Rechab. At dinner, soup as constantly as if I were a Frenchman, an article of my religion learnt in France; meat, one or two sorts, as it may happen, ditto sweet things, of which, with the soup, the principal part of my dinner is composed and the dessert, the frugality matching with that of the dinner. Coffee for anyone that chooses it.[3]

This fascinating invitation to Bentham's strictly regulated establishment at Queen's Square Place, Westminster, was a high honour, as the old man was a notoriously shy personality who accepted the company of but a fairly small circle of intimates. Thompson, however, did not immediately avail himself of the invitation. What he replied we do not know, but on October 28 we find the sage of Queen's Square Place writing mysteriously to the economist, David Ricardo:

T'other day I had to thank you for a letter dated 2nd inst. from my – I will venture to say from our – Hibernian friend. You have, I make no doubt, sympathized with him in his exultation. You will have seen in as strong a light as he and I do, the need there is, that for an indefinite length of time, connections so obnoxious should remain unknown; for all the good he can expect to do may depend on it.[4]

It is, unfortunately, impossible to understand the significance of these allusions, though they undoubtedly refer to Thompson. The philosopher of Utilitarianism later gave instructions for the dispatch to the said Hibernian of copies of his pamphlets *On the Liberty of the Press* and *Letter to Count Toreno*; the postal arrangements were left in the hands of Francis Place, the Radical Tailor of Charing Cross.[5] Then, on May 27, 1822, Bentham learnt through Ricardo that Thompson was expected in England in six weeks' time to make a study of the 'distribution of wealth.' The Irishman arrived in England in the middle of July, and immediately proceeded, on Bentham's advice, to visit the leading educational establishments of the country.

Almost his first visit was to the famous Hazlewood School on the outskirts of Birmingham, which had been founded by Thomas Wright Hill in 1803. The school, the pride of the Utilitarians, was one of the first to be administered by its pupils, who imposed a rigid self-discipline. The constitution and code of laws filled more than a hundred closely printed pages. The pupils elected a committee from among their number to enact and administer the 'laws.' There was a court of justice with schoolboy magistrate, jury, and constables. Thompson records that before visiting the school, though he was aware that the execution of regulations might be left to the pupils, thereby freeing the masters from the odium of imposing punishment, he had not realized that schoolboys could be relied upon, subject to the veto of the head-master, to frame their own regulations. To his eyes, however, 'it seemed rather ludicrous to address a lad of fifteen, acting as judge, with the slavish appellation, "My Lord."' The frequent use of the term 'rank' in a school, as indicating 'something unconnected with merit,' also appeared to him objectionable.

On leaving Hazlewood he went to the home of Bentham, where he remained from October 10, 1822, till February 22, of the following year. He was an intimate member of the household, discussing ideas and mutual interests in the intervals assigned to conversation by his meticulous host. Bentham lent him the manuscript of *Deontology*, his study of ethics, and shared with him the services of his secretary, J. F. Colls, who accompanied him to the Mutual Improvement Society and ordered books for him at Greenlands in Finsbury Square.

During his residence at Queen's Square Place he met the leaders of English Utilitarian thought. Visitors included members of the Hill family; Joseph Hume, the Radical MP, at that time engaged in agitation for the repeal of the Combination Laws; John Black, the editor of the *Morning Chronicle*, London's leading opposition daily; Robert Torrens, the economist; John Bowring, the editor of the Utilitarian *Westminster Review*; James Mill, whose *Elements of Political Economy* had then just appeared; and John Austin the jurist, soon to be appointed Professor of Jurisprudence in the new London University. Foreign reformers and revolutionaries included Hasun el D'Ghies, a progressive Arab serving as Ambassador of Tripoli to the Court of St James; Miranda and Leonotis, revolutionaries from Spanish America and Greece respectively; Blanquière, author of the *History of the Spanish Revolution*, and Marc Antoine Julien, French publicist and editor of the *Revue Encyclopédique*.

During his residence with Bentham, Thompson seems already to have been in contact with Anna Wheeler, in collaboration with whom he was about to write his plea for the emancipation of women bearing the challenging title *Appeal of One Half the Human Race*. Anna Wheeler was a frequent visitor at Queen's Square Place, and about this time the Utilitarian philosopher sent her copies of his books, *Plan of Parliamentary Reform*, *Table of Springs of Action*, *Truth versus Ashurst*, and *Mother Church*.

An amusing description of Thompson during his residence with Bentham, which shows his sense of humour and love of gaiety, is afforded by a letter from Mrs Wheeler's elder daughter, Henrietta, to her younger sister, Rosina, the future wife of the novelist Bulwer Lytton. Henrietta records a conversation which took place in the studio of a Paris sculptor to whom the Utilitarian philosopher was sitting for his portrait. Bentham's two young secretaries were in attendance:

As the conversation happened to fall on Don Tomsono [Henrietta wrote] it is needless to say that the atelier resounded with shouts of laughter, in which even the young artist joined most manfully. After we had alternately related to him all the anecdotes that had fallen under each other's knowledge, one of them exclaimed, 'Oh, but you have not told Miss Wheeler of the Harlequinades!': Whilst he was stopping at *Bentem's*, he was one day with these young men in the library, just equipped for going out – viz., the old plain flannel petticoat about his neck in guise of cloak, and that *séduisant* hat, put on in the true Thompson cock, when they began talking of the agility of harlequin, wherat Thompson immediately said, 'I do declare, by God, that in less than three weeks I could do the same.' 'Well, Mr. Thompson, but you should give us a specimen of your talent.' Whereupon *mio caro uglissimo* gathered his 'auld cloak about him' and hat and all capered, kicked, and frisked and flung about for some time *à la* harlequin, whilst his enlightened and discerning audience were in strong convulsions on the floor. When he was introduced to the young Comte de Miranda, who was complaining that a very short climate incapacitated him from great application to study, Tomsono advanced towards him with a *pas de Zephyr*, and levelling his *tons* at him, told him that this must be caused by a defect in his own intellect. The young man at first stared, but had tact enough to see how matters stood.[6]

In the spring of 1823 Thompson left Queen's Square Place and moved to 81, Great Titchfield Street; his relations with his former host nevertheless remained as close as ever. The two friends continued to be mutually helpful in disseminating each other's ideas. Bentham sent the Irishman his *Laws and Regulations* and his *Leading Principles of a Constitutional Code* and obtained from Thompson the address at Dunmanway, County Cork, of John O'Driscoll, whose book, *Views of Ireland*, had been purchased for him by Bentham's secretary during his residence at Queen's Square Place. A few days later we find Bentham sending Bowring copies of the *Constitutional Code* and the *Mechanics Prospectus* with instructions that they be dispatched to O'Driscoll with other suitable literature.

It is interesting to observe that some of Thompson's most important writing was carried out while he was a guest of the Utilitarian philosopher, and that a curious similarity is to be found in the literary productions of the two authors at this period of their closest intercourse. Bentham at the time was completing his *Leading Principles of a Constitutional Code*, while Thompson was engaged on his major study on the distribution of wealth. Though the two works deal in the main with totally unrelated subjects, the *Constitutional Code* devotes a few brief pages to the distribution of wealth which embody in basic, though at times rudimentary form, many of Thompson's premises and assumptions, almost the whole of his terminology and tools of analysis, a considerable portion of his methodological technique, and even a few of his major conclusions.

Thompson was deeply impressed by the rational basis of Benthamism which confuted the old but widely held thesis that the antiquity of an institution was a proof of its virtue. He regarded it, moreover, as the most hopeful approach yet made toward a scientific examination of society and of human behaviour, declaring that Bentham 'had done more for moral science than Bacon did for physical science.'[7] Above all, the Utilitarian philosopher's famous slogan, 'the greatest good of the greatest number,' evoked the warmest sympathy from the Irishman, who saw in it a golden defence for his own ideal of an equality that would transcend the differences of birth and race, wealth and sex.

But though Thompson remained a lifelong friend and student of his sometime host, he soon decided that his admiration need not force him to accept those aspects of Utilitarianism which the classical economists were shaping into a defence of the market economy. Thus, he broke with the majority of the Utilitarians who accepted Ricardo's wage-fund theory and the Malthusian doctrine of population, and, abandoning the Benthamite belief in *laissez-faire*, he set about developing Utilitarian arguments in defence of the collectivism with which the name of Robert Owen was then becoming associated.

Thompson had first been 'broached by Mr Owen' in 1822 at about the time of the latter's celebrated visit to Ireland, where he had received little short of a royal welcome, debating with doctors of theology at Maynooth College and addressing the Dublin Rotunda on how the population of Ireland could be increased to fifty million, an Archbishop, a Duke, a Lord Mayor, and two Peers being on his platform. Owen's ideas had made little appeal to Thompson in the first heyday of their popularity, appearing to him merely 'an improved system of pauper management,' useful for that purpose but for no other. Owen, moreover, was somewhat suspect on account of his frequent appeals to wealthy and ruling circles. He had interviewed Prince Louis Phillipe and the Prime Minister of France and prepared addresses for the reactionary Lord Castlereagh to lay before the Aix-la-Chapelle Congress of the Great Powers; even after his attacks on religion lost him the support of bishops, his committee had included the Dukes of Kent and Sussex, the elder Peel and the economists, Ricardo, Horne-Tooke, and Torrens. Thompson was instinctively repelled by such courting of royal and aristocratic patronage. He relates:

Such was my love of Freedom and Exertion *in all its consequences*, as opposed to Force and Fraud, whether practised by lawmakers, or those whose actions laws restrained, that I turned away with disgust from a system which then seemed to me to court the patronage of non-representative lawmakers.

He feared that the patronage of the ruling classes would convert knowledge into 'an instrument of mischief, the ally and support of selfish short-sighted interests.'

He was perhaps the first Socialist writer to explain that in the transformation to Socialism class determinism would inevitably turn the rich as a class into the opponents of an equalitarian society. As early as 1822 he wrote:

No high-sounding moral maxims influence or can influence the rich as a body. A few individuals may rise above the impulses of their class ...

These exceptions, able to view impartially matters closely related to themselves, should be 'numbered among the heroes and philosophers of society'; they did not negate the general rule:

> The rich, as a class, like all other classes in every community, must obey the influence of the peculiar circumstances in which they are placed, must acquire the inclinations and the characters, good or bad, which spring out of the state of things surrounding them from their birth.

Though sceptical of Owen's reliance on the rich, Thompson's study of the causes and effects of the distribution of wealth rapidly resulted in his whole-hearted conversion to Co-operation.[8] He explains:

> It was my duty to examine every proposed mode of distribution. Patient study of the system of labour by the Mutual Co-operation of large numbers showed me that all force and fraud were necessarily incompatible with its introduction and support, with its principles and advantages.

After half a year's 'persevering inquiry' he came to the conclusion that Owen's 'mystery and frequent boldness of style,' his 'occasional inaccuracies of reason and statement on subordinate points,' or his failure to consider 'popular objections,' had caused him to be misunderstood by his critics. Not one of the experts in morals, legislation, or political economy who pronounced his system 'impracticable' had 'taken the trouble to examine his arrangements or his mode of execution.' Thompson, for his part, struck up an acquaintance with Owen and soon became convinced that the latter's object 'in courting or seeming to court' the patronage of the despots of Europe was merely to have 'intercourse with the minds of his fellow creatures under their control.'

By this time the Irishman's investigation of the distribution of wealth, for which he had come to England, was well under way and he was writing his 276,000-word *magnum opus*, which was to appear under the title: *An Inquiry into the Principles of the Distribution of Wealth most conducive to Human Happiness, applied to the newly proposed System of Voluntary Equality of Wealth.*

The year 1824, which saw the publication of this book, found the Co-operative Movement in a period of transition and excitement. Owen, who for several years had been proposing the establishment of a community on Co-operative lines, suddenly announced his intention of purchasing 'Harmony,' a settlement in Indiana, USA. The purchase opened a new era in the Co-operative Movement. As the English Co-operators turned their eyes towards the New World, Owen prepared to direct operations from 'New Harmony,' as he re-named it, and to leave the day-to-day control of the British movement in other hands. *An Inquiry into the Principles of the Distribution of Wealth* revealed that in Thompson the Co-operative Movement had acquired a leader who equalled Owen in stature and who offered a refreshingly democratic alternative to the latter's rather arrogant and often dictatorial lead. Moreover, though Thompson was Owen's first important disciple, he soon became the outstanding theoretician of the Co-operative Movement, developing a powerful critique of competitive society which was to have a wide impact on Co-operative and general working-class thought, and which in turn greatly influenced Owen's own political thinking. The teacher, in fact, became the pupil; as Sidney and Beatrice Webb have correctly stated, the sage of New Lanark 'took his economics from his friend William Thompson.'[9]

3

Inquiry into the Distribution of Wealth

Thompson himself tells us of the incident which led him to commence writing his *Inquiry into the Principles of the Distribution of Wealth*,[1] a work which was to render him famous and completely to change his life by drawing him away from agriculture and trade into the centre of Co-operative and Socialist politics. Sometime about 1819 or 1820 he had attended a lecture at one of the Cork literary societies at which:

> a gentleman celebrated for his skill in the controversies of political economy thought fit to descant on the blessings of the *inequality* of wealth, on the dependence and consequent gratitude which the poor should feel to the rich, on the too great freedom and too great equality of wealth in the United States of America.

Thompson was 'astonished at such notions, particularly from such a man.' He replied on the spot, and 'determined to enter into the subject and to lay it before the Society in the shape of an essay for future and more enlarged discussion.' As the essay proceeded the importance and extent of the subject seemed to increase, and the Irish inquirer became more and more aware of 'the confused and erroneous notions prevailing everywhere, in print and conversation'; this redoubled his zeal for 'its completion to whatever extent the interests of truth might require.'[2]

The tragic anomaly of what Thompson termed 'misery in the midst of all the means of happiness' was in his day more evident in Britain than in any other country. It appeared to him, as to so many observers of his time, that 'the productive labourers' were becoming every day 'more productive and more depressed.'[3] The idea of 'increasing misery' haunted him and evoked in his mind a number of disturbing questions:

How comes it that a nation abounding more than any other in the rude materials of wealth, in machinery, dwellings and food, in intelligent and industrious producers, with all the apparent means of happiness, with all the outward semblances of happiness exhibited by a small and rich portion of the community, should still pine in privation?

How comes it that the fruits of the labour of the industrious after years of incessant and successful exertion, are mysteriously and without imputation of fault to them, without any convulsion of nature, swept away?

Why is it that the system enriches a few at the expense of the mass of producers, to make the poverty of the poor more helpless, to throw back the middling classes upon the poor, that a few may be enabled, not only to accumulate in perniciously large masses the national capital, but also by means of such accumulations to command the products of the yearly labour of the community.[4]

He could not accept the idea of Mrs Marcet that inequality was 'necessary to give employment and food to the industrious classes' or that the poor would 'starve if there were not masses of wealth of hundreds of thousands of pounds concentrated in single hands to set the people to work.' Nor could he share the ideal of James Mill, who hoped to see the emergence of a growing middle class exempt from 'the necessity of any bodily labour for its support, possessed in a moderate degree of the comforts and conveniences of life' and capable of devoting its time to literature, cultured life, and happiness.

He expressed the hope that his book would help to spread a knowledge of social science among a wider population. Hitherto it had been examined only in 'the calm closets of philosophical inquirers, where it delighted and elevated only the minds of a few.' If it could be widely diffused it would be of practical use to all mankind, and would expunge from science the stain which Condorcet had pointed out when he declared that it had done much for the glory, but little or nothing for the happiness of mankind.

Social science was the focus whereat the various branches of knowledge converged, and where they could most successfully be utilized for the creation of human happiness. Moralists were ignorant of physical science and of political economy; theologians 'affected to disdain all other knowledge but their own peculiar and profitable dreams'; political economists drew 'a broad line of distinction between their solid material speculations and the airy philosophy of the mind' and 'professed to direct their sole attention to the production and accumulation of wealth, regardless of its distribution, leaving moralists, politicians and statesmen to consider its effect on happiness'; chemists, mechanics, manufacturers, and merchants disdained the speculations of political economists as 'mere theories,' inapplicable to the realities of their respective operations. This fragmentation of knowledge should be corrected, for there was no hope of progress as long as the science of morals remained divorced from that of political economy. The distribution of wealth should be studied from both points of view; if a contradiction appeared between them, it must not be ignored but resolutely faced and a remedy sought.

The primary object of the *Inquiry* was to examine which distribution of wealth would achieve the greatest happiness of the greatest number as well as the greatest production. It sought to solve the 'cruel dilemma' of how 'to reconcile just distribution with continued production,' to trace the various economic, social, and moral effects of various possible distributions of wealth, and, finally, 'to point out those just and gentle means'[5] by which the good society could be achieved and perpetuated.

Distribution, Thompson insisted, was the basic problem of social science: 'no subject was more interesting, or, if rightly treated, more useful.' On it directly depended 'not only the physical comforts of every community, but, consequently, in a very great degree, the quantum of morality as well as of intellectual enjoyment within its reach.'[6] Happiness and unhappiness, morality and immorality, vice and virtue, all sprang directly from the economic system and the nature of the ownership of property. 'To speak of morals and legislation with an affected contempt for such matters' was 'to grasp at a shadow and to leave a substance,' for 'the radical defect in the constitution of society' was 'the excessive inequality of wealth':

> Wherever this radical evil is permitted to exist, no free institutions, no just laws can be made, or if made, can long be supported. Without it, titles and aristocracy could be stripped of their false clothing, and would be so ridiculous that their owners even would be ashamed to wear them.[7]

To attempt the huge task of bringing the problem of the optimum distribution of wealth into the sphere of social science, Thompson developed an analysis which may be termed 'moral economy.' As W.

Stark has observed, Thompson's underlying belief was that economics should be 'both realistic and idealistic; realistic in describing and analysing the actual order of society, idealistic in announcing and advocating the perfect nature underlying it, the order that should prevail.'[8]

The first half of the *Inquiry* argues from the assumption that in the then existing state of human nature pure equality was incompatible with the maximum production of wealth, and that it had somehow to be synthesized with the labourer's right to the full fruit of his toil. In contrast to this ideal, Thompson describes the existing system, the inequalities of which he indicts in passionate language.

In the second half of the book he adopts a new approach and urges there is no need to assume that 'moral wisdom could not so improve' as to render perfect equality possible. He emphasizes the importance of Robert Owen's experiment at the New Lanark cotton mills, which Owen claimed had proved the existence of other incentives to production beside fear of starvation and love of riches. On the basis of this experience Owen had asserted that almost all falsehood, violence, and stealing proceeded from inequality of wealth, and had virtually been abolished at his mills. Realizing to the full the revolutionary significance of these claims, Thompson made this triumphant comment: 'he would certainly be no mean benefactor to his species who could demonstrate the practicability of thoroughly eradicating these most numerous miseries and vices.'[9] Owen's system would work, he argued, because by destroying the exploitation of man it would terminate a system of 'plunder and inequality' most inimical to incentive. If 'motives equally or more efficient than those arising from personal gain' could be 'put into operation to ensure an equally large production,' social motives 'ought to be preferred to selfish ones.'[10] To defend this proposition he devoted the last 200 pages of the *Inquiry* to a careful investigation of the advantages of Co-operation as against 'labour by individual competition.'*

---

* The *Inquiry* notes mysteriously that its fifth chapter 'consisting of about one hundred pages' has been 'withheld' for the convenience of publication and lest it 'lead to unnecessary and otherwise unavoidable irritation.' What happened to these 'missing pages' and what they contained has long mystified Thompson's readers; the present writer, who conducted an exhaustive search for them in vain, is of the opinion that they are lost in the sands of time but that Thompson used a considerable portion of them in preparing his later work *Labour Rewarded*.

Thompson's masterpiece had a decisive impact on the entire Co-operative Movement, in which it was widely read and frequently quoted. Robert Owen was deeply impressed by the work; he had it distributed at his own expense by Messrs Wheatley and Alard in the Strand, and took a large number of copies with him when he sailed for America to establish the New Harmony community. During the voyage he read from it to his fellow passengers, and on arrival he read extracts and distributed copies to vast audiences, presenting copies to many distinguished Americans, among them the editor of the *Pennsylvania National Gazette*.[11] John Minter Morgan welcomed the *Inquiry* in a series of Co-operative allegories, and pronounced it 'the most able work upon Political Economy since Adam Smith's *Wealth of Nations*.'[12] He observed that Thompson was the first to coin the word 'competitive' to describe the existing economic system; bourgeois circles dared not face his exposure of 'the sophistry and errors' of the 'infatuated school of economists,' who pretended 'to teach a simple science,' yet contrived to 'mystify every question relating to human happiness and social improvement.' In a supposed conversation with 'Atticus,' Minter Morgan prophesied the ultimate triumph of Thompson's ideas:

Neglected Thompson, whose attainment towers
Beyond the reach of critics' feebler powers
And vain attempts his reasoning to refute,
Has taught them wisdom – for behold them mute.
But when this weaker generation's past
And struggling truths, unfetter'd, rise at last,
Then shall his work transcendent be confess'd
And distant nations by his genius bless'd.

The *Inquiry* was warmly welcomed throughout the Co-operative Press. Owen's *Crisis* eulogized it in passionate language in an open letter to Earl Grey, Lord Brougham, and Viscount Melbourne, while in America the Co-operative journal *Phosphor* declared that 'what Lavoisier did in chemistry, William Thompson and Robert Owen are likely to produce in Association.' Belfast Co-operators drank a toast in coffee to the 'enlightened author of the *Inquiry*.' In America members of the Owenite New Harmony community assembled on Sundays to hear 'lessons' from it read out by the Editor of the *New Harmony Gazette*.[13] On the periphery of the movement many copies of

Thompson's book were purchased by the London Working Man's Club and various Mechanics Institutes.[14] W. Longson of Stockport declared it was 'an invaluable masterpiece written by one of the greatest philanthropists of the present or any past age.'[15] The French socialist Lechevalier referred to its author as one of the leading opponents of the competitive system.[16]

4

The Ideal Principles of Distribution

Like Marx after him, Thompson rejected the belief of the orthodox economists that economics should avoid making a value judgment, and insisted that the existing system must not be regarded as either immutable or sacrosanct. He held that present or past distributions of wealth, like old-fashioned methods of making windmills, deserved systematic study; that this was 'a matter of history,' useful information without which would be to 'work without tools' or to 'build without materials'; 'but neither the tools nor the materials were the finished fabric.'

His position, he declared, was intermediate between that of the 'airy' political philosophers and the 'materialism' of the orthodox economists (who had not yet taken up welfare economics). He regarded political philosophers like Godwin as altogether unrealistic 'intellectual spectators.' Because their own 'animal wants' were comfortably supplied, they paid little attention to the material wants of others, considering man 'capable of attaining happiness by his mental powers alone, *almost* independent of material subordinate agency'; they affected to disdain labour as 'mechanical and grovelling,' and often allied themselves with the political aristocracy.[1] They forgot that without the aid of labour their 'high intellectual energies could scarcely for one hundred hours preserve themselves.'

The 'mechanical speculators,' on the other hand, went to the other extreme. They thought that intellectual power and sympathy formed no part of the creature man, that he was altogether a mechanical agent, like the plough or the loom, and that he had to be urged to labour by the same rude means that were used for other animals. Such 'sublime ideas' as intelligence, benevolence, mutual co-operation, and the perfectibility of man were derided because the sole objective was assumed to be the maximization of production; to the economists it mattered not:

24

By what means or by whom the articles were produced, whether by camels, horses, men, slaves or not slaves, whether by hard labour or easy labour, by healthful or life-consuming exertion, signified not, except in as far as the wear and tear of the dead or living machinery might enhance the price and lessen production.

By what means or by whom articles were consumed whether by the mass of producers to diffuse gladness through a smiling population, or by a few living in palaces surrounded by unenjoyed waste and sickly appetites, signified not.

Thompson rejected the 'intellectual' conceptions of Godwin and the 'materialism' of the orthodox economists, arguing that man was neither 'a mere machine' nor 'a mere intellectual agent'; he was 'a complicated being.' Without a constant realizing of this fact:

the regulating principle of *utility* is sacrificed, and the grand object of political economy, the indefinite increase of wealth, becomes worthless. Three-fourths or nine-tenths of the human race are consigned to the wretchedness of unrequited toil so that the remaining smaller portion may pine in indolence midst unenjoyed profusion.

Thompson's analysis of the 'rights' of distribution makes the Benthamite assumption that it is necessary to seek the greatest good of the greatest number, and follows the classical economists in postulating that labour is the sole producer of wealth. The discussion centres around two basic principles of distribution – equality and the right of the labourer to the full fruit of his toil. Thompson's ideas seem to have been systematized by his association with Bentham, whose underlying contention that the science of distribution could possess 'the character and certainty of a mathematical proportion,' he shared. He agreed with the Utilitarian philosopher also in assuming that the capacity of different persons to enjoy happiness must be considered as equal because it was not possible of measurement.

Bentham had postulated four basic 'principles of distribution': subsistence, abundance, security, and equality; but had speedily dismissed the first two as of little importance, and had gone on to discuss whether or not there must be 'constant opposition and eternal war' between security and equality. Thompson followed him in much of his analysis, but with another end in view. For while in the main Bentham had sought to ensure the security of the property-owner, Thompson was primarily concerned with that of the worker, and therefore found it much less difficult than Bentham to equate equality with security. The difference between the ideas of the two writers may be illustrated by their attitude toward the question of Negro slavery; the Utilitarian philosopher contended that emancipation should be 'gradual' so as not to endanger 'security of property,' while Thompson declared that the slave-owner's right to security must be subordinated to the slave's more important right to freedom. The gulf between them is again revealed by their proposals for modifying the glaring inequalities of the social system, Bentham's solution being the imposition of death duties, while Thompson's aimed at a revolution in property relationships.

Thompson declared that it was because human beings could enjoy happiness infinitely more than animals that they had the right to obtain paramount influence for themselves and their interests.[2] If anyone could prove that his organism so excelled that of his fellow men as to enable him to experience infinitely greater happiness than the rest of his species, his claim, like that of man above the oyster, ought to be allowed, and wealth and all other means of happiness ought to be applied to him in greater measure than to others. The mental powers of the race were, however, highly mutable; if neglected, they were 'little superior to those of the ape,' while if cultivated, they excelled 'what poets feigned of the minds and morals of the old immortal gods.' The same was true of variations in capacity for physical enjoyment, but since these differences were environmental they were irrelevant to the discussion. When differences were innate, as in the case of taste, they were relatively trifling. If the attempt were made to calculate the capacity for happiness of various individuals how would allowance be made for the changes that continuously take place through age or illness? How could the capacity of different individuals be gauged? Who could be trusted to undertake such tests without claiming that any exceptions to a rule of equality should be made in his or her own favour? Should the measurers be the rich or the poor, the young or the old, the studious or the illiterate? The wise and the good would hardly wish to benefit themselves at the expense of others; if they did, they would soon cease to be wise and good. Moreover, if wisdom and morality were to be the criterion 'who would not put in his claim for these qualities?' To pose these questions was to render it self-evident that:

> to us inequalities in the capacity for enjoyment *do not exist*, because they are by us inappreciable; they cannot enter into our moral and

political calculations for they can no more than the galvanic fluid be seized and measured.

The only fair method of measuring need would be a majority vote, but the majority would 'naturally' determine in its own favour and opt for 'the greatest good of the greatest number,' which in practice would mean equality. This would benefit the whole community by avoiding the selfishness, jealousy, and rancour which were born of inequality.

Following lines Bentham had already sketched out, Thompson developed another important argument for equality, declaring that a unit of wealth would produce more happiness if transferred from a richer to a poorer person:

> Such is the effect on happiness of the continued addition of successive equal portions of wealth that every succeeding portion diminishes in effect. Of 1,000 portions of the matter of wealth, the first 100 are necessary to repel hunger and thirst and to support life. The use of this first portion is as life to death; the value is the greatest of all human values, including the capacity for all other enjoyments, for which nature or education may have adapted the individual. What is the effect on the same individual of the application of a second mass, say of a hundred, of these portions of wealth: nothing ecstatic, no change as from life to death; simply the addition of some of the most obvious comforts of life demanded by real convenience. The effect of these second hundred in intensity of enjoyment is so infinitely beneath that produced by the first 100, as to be incapable of any comparison. Every hundred added is less and less productive of absolute increase of happiness to the possessor; the difference of effect of each addition is less and less.[3]

It was evident, Thompson continued, that equalization of property would wonderfully increase the happiness-producing power of each portion of wealth, even if the 'glittering magnificence' of accumulated wealth were thereby to disappear. Like Godwin, he argued that most opponents of equality were biased in that they themselves benefited from inequality. It was often declared that without inequality there would be no works of splendour and magnificence, no institutions of learning, and no modes of faith, but if anything were found to militate against happiness it should not be maintained.[4] Display was the parent of envy, and superseded all pleasurable feelings of sympathy, while the pleasures of vanity which it produced soon palled. Inequality, moreover, resulted in crime and immorality, which invariably centred around the possession of wealth. Those who claimed that equality was against Divine injunction merely imputed 'malignity to God,' for whatever was best for human happiness 'must be most pleasing to a benevolent being.' No religion needed the support of inequality if it was of value. Intellectual pleasures also were reduced rather than increased by excessive inequality of wealth, the more so as useful discoveries were almost always made by 'persons in moderate or lowly circumstances,' and not by the very rich.

Thompson was utterly opposed to the veneration for precedent which Blackstone and Burke invoked to sanctify long-established institutions. He declared that institutions 'must be considered as mere means' for the 'promotion of the greatest happiness'; the more ancient an institution which stood in the way of happiness, the more misery it had caused, and the sooner it should be removed.

These arguments, which provide a classic defence of equality, were enthusiastically taken up by the Co-operative Movement; egalitarianism was the order of the day with Co-operative Societies in London, the provinces, and New York. At the Scots community of Orbiston 'about two-thirds of the members' subscribed to egalitarianism, though a vocal minority declared themselves opposed to Thompson's ideas.

Thompson's second principle of distribution was the worker's right to the whole produce of labour, a doctrine in Professor Foxwell's view of 'great revolutionary power and political significance.' The *Distribution of Wealth* accepts the Benthamite argument that security is a *sine qua non* of production, but argues that it must not be a principle 'favouring the rich alone'; for though the economists and the propertied classes assumed that security was synonymous with the existence of privileges and excessive wealth, the labourer was the sole producer of wealth and the person most in need of security.[5]

Extraction from the product of labour was at its worst under the system of slavery in which labour was least productive, most 'immorally oppressed' and most unhappy.[6] The evil had not, however, been eradicated under capitalism, for therein the labourer's right to the whole of his produce was denied by the classes who had appropriated the land and materials necessary for production. These classes sanctimoniously clamoured for 'security' and proclaimed that 'no atom of any article of wealth should under any pretext be taken from its possessor' by force, yet all the while they did their utmost 'to deceive and induce, to terrify and compel the productive labourer to work for the *smallest possible portion* of the produce of his labour.'

Thompson considered it was the duty of the legislators to take heed of the motives which govern production, not to interfere with them. 'Any mode of distribution unfriendly to continued and increasing production' was 'like a child gnawing the entrails of the parent that produced it.' Security should therefore be administered impartially to all, and one producer should never be robbed to encourage another. Once the principle of 'security' was compromised the labourer's incentive to produce was diminished and an inroad effected which could not be halted; there would be 'no other limit to it than the caprice of the rapacious.'[7]

History showed that incentive could not be replaced by naked force or superstition. In proportion as the reward of productive labour fell 'the efforts of industry' were relaxed, 'till at length, at their extreme point of apathy,' brute force had to be used 'to extort, by means of terror, a reluctant produce from the arms of wretchedness.' Unless the labourer's right to his products was acknowledged 'it would be folly' for him 'to produce them; they would cease to be produced.'

Under capitalism the workers were forced by the 'stimulus of immediate want' to labour for the lowest possible rate. This did not add to their alacrity or skill. On the contrary, their employers were self-punished. 'They calculated that whatever could be saved from the labourers would go to enrich themselves.' This might have been the case if 'man were a machine, like the loom, uninfluenced by moral causes,' but, being more 'subtle' than the machine, when deprived of the produce of his toil he became dissatisfied, careless, and hopeless, because he knew the produce was for another. It became his fixed policy to idle and do bad work.[8]

Coupled in Thompson's mind with the idea of labour's 'security over its produce' was the concept of 'voluntary exchange.' He argues that the hampering of free exchanges was the same as an attack on 'security' in that it annihilated the motives to labour. Exchanges were valuable because they made possible the division of labour, widened the interest of the individual, and made him more sympathetic, less selfish and isolated. Forced exchanges, on the other hand, generated ill will and destroyed incentive to produce. If a misguided producer were assumed to have overestimated the value of his produce, it should not be too difficult to make him see reason.[9]

Thompson had thus shown, on the one hand, that happiness would be maximized if an equal distribution were achieved, and on the other, that it was necessary to guarantee the labourer's right to the whole product of his toil if maximum production were to be ensured. Like Bentham, he was now faced with the problem of reconciling these two principles.

Equality, he had explained, was 'calculated to produce incalculably more happiness than any other mode of distribution.' The principle would have been 'irresistible' were it not for the fact that wealth could not be produced without labour and that the exigencies of production introduced 'a limitation to equality.'[10]

'What shall we do?' he cries. 'Shall we renounce the blessings of equality as ideal, but not applicable to the real state of things?' By no means:

> First, the rule of equality must be followed where no labour is employed in production.
>   Second, wherever a departure is made from the principle of 'securing to everyone the free use of his labour and its products, that departure should always be in favour of equality.[11]

Thompson explains that though equality and security were 'mortal enemies' under existing conditions, they were not necessarily so. Inequality of wealth and 'all its train of physical evils' were not due in capitalist society to 'differences in the productivity of different labourers' but to the relationship between employer and employed. 'No fortune had ever been or ever could be accumulated by mere individual production'; on the contrary, 'forcible seizure and fraudulent exchange' had been 'the only efficient means of acquiring large masses of wealth.'[12] True security would therefore be 'the friend of equality,' and the two principles coincided to such an extent that 'the greatest quantity of the one' led 'to the greatest quantity of the other.'[13]

Thompson, like Godwin and Bentham, was reluctant to employ force to achieve his goal. He warned the labourer against seizing back his property from those who had usurped it, arguing that if he employed violence he would annihilate his own claim to 'security,' not only to the entire use, but to any use of what his labour had created.[14] Force would 'annihilate production,' for though equality pleaded 'altogether in favour of the productive labourer,' security stood neuter, prohibiting compulsion to either party. Violence would lead to economic waste and the brutalization of character; the loser would smart from injustice, and the gainer from an uneasy conscience. Contrary to the proverb stolen waters were not sweet, and bread eaten in secret was not pleasant. Even a minor abstraction would excite alarm and make the whole community feel 'insecure.' It was better to make a big abstraction from one rich man than smaller ones from many, but to attempt this would usually be found impracticable.[15]

Thompson seemed willing, temporarily at least, to write off the property hitherto acquired by the rich. It was most important, he considered, to ensure that all future creations of wealth should remain in the possession of their real producers. Though at first view the immense accumulations of wealth produced by past exploitation seemed to 'render hopeless any approximation to equality,' the removal of restraints was a necessary first step 'to give fair play to human exertion'; unless exploitation were stopped, it would be of no avail to increase the powers of production. The actual accumulations of the past were 'very small' compared with the potentialities of production. If the labourer recovered 'the entire use of the products of his labour' great fortunes could no longer be built up, for all newly created wealth would belong to the workers who produced it. The handful of past accumulations might therefore be left in the possession of existing owners, though it could be redistributed if that increased the happiness of the community. The minority who owned such accumulations would in any case ultimately be persuaded to relinquish them, and, 'whether convinced or not,' would be induced to 'conform to the clearly expressed wishes of those around them,' the more so as they would 'find no other use for their capital,' and they would have no claim to their property in a society which accepted the 'nullity of original right.' The fact that a man owned 'a piece of land or a quantity of silver or brass or gold' should give him no right to determine what should be done with these possessions after his death; the right of bequest was as absurd as the claim to control the disposal of property a thousand years hence.[16]

5

Exploitation

Of central importance in the *Inquiry into the Distribution of Wealth* is the analysis of how the worker in competitive society is denied the whole product of his labour, and why so large a proportion of the national revenue is consumed by apparently unproductive capitalists and landlords. This discussion was not new in Thompson's day: in the three previous decades it had received growing attention from William Godwin, Charles Hall, and Piercy Ravenstone in England, and from Simonde de Sismondi in France. Thompson is far more emphatic, however, in his assertions that the 'idle classes' have no right to share in the national product, and that exploitation is the basic characteristic of capitalism and the source of the greater part of its ills. Unlike the earlier writers, who had merely criticized existing society without proposing a definite alternative, Thompson fused his critique with advocacy of Owen's Co-operative proposals.

His analysis opened by closely following Ricardo's *Principles of Political Economy*, which had appeared some seven years earlier. Thompson explained that the value of an article did not depend on its desirability, its rarity, its utility, or its beauty; but upon the labour which produced it. Wealth was in fact 'produced by labour' without which an 'article of desire' could not be 'converted into an article of wealth.'

Like Ricardo, he sought to expound the theory of value in two distinctly different ways. He considered that in most cases value could be measured by the amount of labour employed in production. Where, however, long-term competitive conditions were not operative and the supply of a commodity was restricted, another method of assessing value was required. In considering a well, for example, its value would be determined not by the labour of digging it, but by the labour 'otherwise necessary to bring water there from its nearest supply.' Imported articles might be valued not by the labour employed in making them abroad, but by the labour required to manufacture them at home. The value of building land must be assessed not by the labour actually employed in clearing it, but by the labour saved in carriage and other-wise. When new land began to force down the value of old land with which it competed, the labour which had originally been expended became, so to speak, retrospectively misdirected and in consequence lost.[1]

The price of pleasure grounds did not really depend on the competing desires of the rich but on the labour involved in production; for if new grounds could be produced, the labour employed in laying them out would be the measure of their value. If their supply was in any way restricted they had 'a surplus value of their own,' but it was – and here Thompson's analysis departs from that of Ricardo – a surplus value which 'could scarcely have place, or but to a very small extent, under the natural, unconstrained and most useful distribution of wealth' toward which society was approaching. Similarly, the valu-ation of 'superfluous trinkets, without use and sought after only by the savage and the courtier,' embodied 'mere artificial value' not worthy of consideration. Under 'representative self-government' they would no longer be regarded as objects 'conferring merit' and would fall to 'their true commercial value, the value of real use.'

Thompson conceded that labour was not 'in all cases an accurate measure,' as desires and preferences were 'apt to vary' with physical and moral circumstances, and with the quantum of knowledge and the means of converting to use the materials and energies of nature. What he asserted, however, was that in any given state of society, with any given desires and at any particular time, labour was the sole measure of value, and, under such circumstances, an accurate measure. To search for a measure which would hold good amid changing desires, tastes, and methods of production, was to 'hunt after a shadow'; for what at one time was an object of wealth might at another be a mere object of desire, and might subsequently even cease to be that. Labour, on the other hand, was always an essential of production and a source of value; for though there were tribes by whom 'neither corn, nor cotton, nor wool, nor gold, nor rice, nor silver' were esteemed articles of wealth, there were no human beings by whom human labour was not esteemed an article of value. It was in fact the only universal commodity.

To the argument that greater skill is exerted in one species of work more than in another, or by one labourer more than another, Thompson replied, as did all the theoreticians of the labour theory, that all labour was 'resolvable' into the 'ordinary' work of the community. If an individual accomplished in two days what ordinary skill or untaught skill could accomplish in four, that labour was double the value of ordinary labour: if labour were inefficiently carried out it had similarly to be scaled down in any calculations that might be made. Labour must therefore be conceived in terms of 'ordinary skill and diligence'; other circumstances, such as danger, noxious smells, moisture, cold, and extra exertion involved in production, ought also to be taken into consideration.

Having established that labour is the sole source of wealth, Thompson proceeds to argue that there can therefore be no other source for profits. Developing an argument which Godwin and others had already suggested he claimed that:

> the materials, the buildings, the machinery, the wages, can add nothing to their own value. ... The spade may as well be called the parent of grain, instead of the laborious arm that wields it, as any of these articles constituting capital can be called the parents of the manufactured article.[2]

Capital was 'the mere creature of labour and materials,' not their creator.'[3] 'The dead material is nothing; the active mind and hand are the sole objects of philosophical and moral regard.'[4]

Rich lands were sometimes declared a source of wealth; but 'what was their value until they had been cleared and brought into cultivation by labour?'[5]

> Originally the land was valueless; only labour had made it valuable. The first settler cleared the timber, erected a shed and affixed the value of his labour to that part of the soil on which it had been expended and to those contiguous spots rendered by it more convenient for use. A second settler, paying for the labour under the name of the land, added to its value by expending more labour upon it, clearing a larger space, cultivating useful crops, improving the sheds and perhaps rearing and domesticating some animals. A third settler pays an increased value for all these products of labour under the name of the soil to which they are attached, introduces stock and machines, all produced by labour, and leaving the former erections for subordinate or temporary purposes, erects houses and makes fences suited for permanence and convenience. Thus is a piece of land, which was a few years ago an object of no value, now converted

into an object of wealth. What has nature done towards this conversion? Nothing. What has man, what has man's labour done? Everything.

But though labour was the sole producer of wealth, it was the idle owners of the means of production who obtained the lion's share of the produce of labour. 'Two measures' for the division of wealth were theoretically possible: The labourer considered that the owner or superintendent of capital should be given an allowance for the depreciation of his capital 'with such added compensation as would support him in equal comfort with the more actively employed labourers.' The capitalist, on the other hand, demanded that he should be allowed to appropriate 'the additional value' produced by the use of his 'machinery or other capital,' claiming that he should enjoy 'the whole of such surplus value' as a reward for 'his superior intelligence and skill' in accumulating it and advancing it to the labourers.

The difference between the two measures was 'immense': one meant 'almost perfect equality,' the other 'excess of wealth and poverty.'[6] The labourer's 'measure' could not be achieved without 'universal diffusion of knowledge and justice,' though the 'tendency' had been to move nearer it as force and fraud were removed by the progress of economic development. Nevertheless, wherever it had been possible to exploit the working class, 'the largest quantity' that could be 'withdrawn from every labourer' had been 'the only limit' to such extractions; the worker 'stript of all capital' had found his wages forced down to the lowest rate 'compatible with the existence of industrious habits.' 'Defalcations' from the earnings of labour had varied with circumstances, but on average had amounted to 'at least one half the products of labour,' and that when capital was 'most abundant and competition among capitalists most active.'[7]

The economists were wrong to assume that profits and the rate of interest depended mainly on the amount of wealth accumulated in a community; whatever the amount accumulated, if it all remained in the hands of the producers, the price demanded for the occasional use of any portion of it would be low, while if it was monopolized by capitalists the price of the use of it would be very high on account of 'the immense competition' to obtain it.[8] Capitalists in fact promoted foreign wars to prevent the growth of capital from lowering the rate of interest; they then invested in war loans and shared in the proceeds of taxation wrung by the State from the labour of the rest of the community.[9]

The basic fact in 'civilized society' was that the labourer found 'everything around him appropriated'; there was nothing to make his labour productive unless he was prepared to pay tribute to a landlord or capitalist.[10] Such a situation was unknown in primitive society:

> The savage has all the materials of nature, unused around him, to work up. Are there minerals, plants, or animals within his reach affording the materials for clothing, food, tools, shelter or other conveniences? He has only to put out his hand and gather them, and transform them by labour into consumable or exchangeable wealth.

In 'civilized' society, however,

> All the materials to work upon are appropriated by previous labour, force, or fraud; not a piece of stone containing any iron or any useful metal, not a branch of a tree, not a skin of any animal, no rude material that can be turned to any use for food, clothes or covering or any purpose subservient to convenience, that is not already obedient to an owner. Even the very mountain bristling with rocks and repelling the tools and the toils of cultivation is fenced round by the claims of ownership.

Under such conditions:

> the owner of the land comes forward and says he will not insist on an equivalent in labour for the purchase of his land; but he will be satisfied with disposing of the yearly use of it, getting in return every year so much labour, measured by its products, so much of the increase of the soil as may be deemed an equivalent. The owners of the raw materials make a similar claim. Sometimes even the owner of the tools to work with, if they be very complicated and costly or require permanent fixtures, makes a similar demand on the unprovided labourers; and even those who possess the food that the labourers must consume until the product of their labour is in a state for consumption or exchange demand a profit.[11]

The result is that:

> The idle possessor of the inanimate instruments of production not only secures to himself by their possession as much enjoyment as the

most diligent and skilful of the real, efficient producers, but in proportion to the amount of his accumulations, by whatever means acquired, he procures ten times, a hundred times, a thousand times as much of the articles of wealth, the products of labour, and means of enjoyment, as the utmost labour of such efficient producers can procure for them.[12]

Thompson echoed Adam Smith in emphasizing that 'a universal and always vigilant conspiracy of capitalists' existed everywhere to cause the labourers to toil for the lowest possible wages and to wrest as much as possible from the produce of their labour.[13] The capitalists, moreover, seized the State power, or, where despotism was too powerful, made the best terms they could with the despot and then affected to find glory in their slavishness to him.[14] They kept 'the mass of the community ignorant, and directly or indirectly monopolized the command of the armed forces, the offices of judges, priests, and all the executive departments which gave the most power, required the least trouble, and rendered the largest pecuniary return.'[15] History had shown that they usurped the power of throwing on to the other classes the burden of taxation and the cost of supporting sinecures for the rich, as well as an administration from which they alone benefited; 'the whole system of human regulations,' though proclaimed in the name of 'rights' and 'privileges,' was 'little more than a tissue of restraints of one class over another.'[16]

From this analysis of exploitation Thompson concluded that nine-tenths of attainable human production and ninety-nine hundredths of possible human happiness would never be brought into existence as long as one set of men possessed productive labour powers alone and another possessed 'the means of putting those powers into operation.' As long as the opposing interests of capital and labour were suffered to exist, the propertyless majority would be robbed and oppressed by the tiny minority who owned the means of production and whose interest was 'always and necessarily' opposed to that of the worker. As long as the labourer was divested of 'everything but the mere power of producing' he would remain 'deprived of almost all the products of his labour' and 'the happiness of the whole human race would be sacrificed, if necessary, in the estimation of the capitalists, to produce an additional quarter per cent profit.'[17]

6

Critique of Competition

Thompson's critique of competitive society was perhaps the first sustained attack on competition produced in the English language, being written at a time when Sismondi and Saint-Simon – to both of whom it owed much – were almost the only students of social and economic affairs who refused to bow to the emergent individualist system. The *Inquiry* was important in that it set the tone of anti-capitalist thought in the British Isles for later decades and laid the foundation for Socialist criticism of capitalism for a long time to come.

Thompson assailed the view that the profit motive was the only incentive to production, urging on the contrary that the honour of being a good workman was usually incentive enough. Most works of art, discoveries, and inventions had been prompted by the best motives, and, even in the case of manual labour, workers were usually afforded a fixed wage irrespective of their actual productivity. Capitalism, however, made selfishness and materialism the leading motives in life. Everyone sought to amass 'his own individual pile,' and there was 'a constant temptation to sacrifice the interest of others.' "Get wealth, if possible honestly; but at all events get wealth!" became the established maxim of society.' Nothing in life was too sacred not to find its price in money. All qualities, moral or intellectual, which did not immediately tend to the increase of wealth, were neglected or treated with scorn as 'appendages of poverty and unfashionable intruders.'[1]

Suspicion engendered by competition prevented the spread of knowledge; there was constant opposition to technological progress on the part of sectional interests who feared that it might render them redundant, and even he who was 'doing well in his calling was interested in concealing his success.' Closely following Sismondi, Thompson claimed that the entrepreneur was often unable to judge whether a market, 'frequently at a great distance, sometimes in another hemisphere,' was overstocked or likely to require the article which he had decided to produce. An error of judgment, however well-intentioned, might 'end in severe distress, if not in ruin.' Reliance on the profit motive entailed periodic trade depressions, with consequent unemployment; labour, though 'teeming with the capabilities of making millions happy,' was obliged to remain dormant. The workers, divorced from the means of making their labour productive, were obliged to compete against each other, thus intensifying their degradation.[2]

Capitalism inevitably divided society into rich and poor, employers and employed. The rich could have no intercourse with the poor, by whose very breath they would not allow themselves to be contaminated, while the poor could hardly associate with them, for a day's pastime of a rich man would involve a poor man in ruin for life.[3]

The rich were wealthy parasites whose desire for ostentation and prestige misdirected production. They demanded glossy furniture, fantastic apartments, the obsequious attendance of servants, and other goods and services to pamper their appetite and gratify their sickly wants. Their lives were an alternation of listlessness and feverish, mostly sensual, excitement; and their consumption was almost complete waste; at times, for example, it took the form of eating in five minutes the fruit of a hundred days' work. Moreover, being based on caprice and not on utility, it was always changing; fashion might decree cashmere shawls one year, pearls another, and diamonds a third; there were therefore continuous trade fluctuations, and consequent uncertainty of unemployment.[4]

From their very infancy the rich had been accustomed to command and receive deference from all around them. Since they had always possessed wealth without labour, they looked upon it as their right and their family's right always to possess it on the same terms. They looked down on the productive labourers, mistakenly assuming that 'the great end of human society' was to maintain themselves in their immense possessions. Their ruling object was the perpetuation and increase of their wealth, but since they despised work, they sought to accomplish it by seizing on political power. 'Nobility, priestcraft, and all similar institutions' were but instruments, 'varied according to time and circumstances,' to perpetuate the power of the rich and to repress the rest of the community. Politically the owners of the means of production were so powerful that even in democratic countries supposed equality in face of the law was a farce. Their interest was always diametrically opposed to that of the rest of the community, and though they might fling away their wealth on luxuries and trifles, they obstinately refused to make the slightest concession to the necessities of others. They even made a distinction between their 'debts of honour,' or obligations which had to be paid to members of their own class, and tradesmen's debts which could be ignored with impunity.[5]

The conflicting interests of employers and employed, and the heterodoxy of the various sectional interests of competitive society, divided and subdivided the moral sanction and necessitated the use of force to keep the web of society together. Men were degraded into the automata of arbitrary regulations:

> Whenever the workers challenged the interests of capital they found themselves confronted by the fact that the employers had influence in making the laws while they had none. New restrictions, new penal laws, more barbarous and absurd than the preceding, are enacted; the producers take measures to defeat these iniquitous laws; they endeavour by a counterforce to make head against the violences instituted against them; they resort to plots and combinations of violence to defeat the power which seeks under the name of law to repress for ever their spirit, and with it their industry. They endeavour by unjust violence towards their own numbers and sullen threats against their employers to keep down the depressing competition of low wages. Thus is a community converted into a theatre of war: hostile camps of the employers and labourers are everywhere formed.[6]

The exploiters claimed that their lives were necessary, as by their consumption they gave employment to the poor, but 'to assert that labourers could not make houses for themselves, tools for themselves, machines for themselves, without the aid of some jugglers stepping in and appropriating them to themselves' was 'a proposition too absurd, when put in plain terms, to admit of refutation.' It was an 'insulting, pernicious absurdity' to assert that the rich supported the poor, for they gave them nothing; every article of wealth consumed by the unproductive classes was really 'so much annual loss to the producers.' If the claim of the rich that their extravagant consumption benefited the poor were conceded, would not an ape capable of consuming ten times as much as the rich man be regarded as still more useful and patriotic?[7]

Capitalism treated the worker, the only productive factor in society, as little more than an animal on a farm, the only difference between the two was that with the decline of slavery the dominant class had contracted out of the obligation of keeping its servants alive. This was perhaps as well, for if workers, like horses, lived at the expense of the capitalist there would doubtless have been 'Ukases, or Acts of Parliament, complaining of the grievance, and providing an equally summary and economical mode of exit' for them. Capitalism provided no insurance against accidents, sickness, or old age. Even the voluntary compensation schemes, first proposed by the 'celebrated' Condorcet, were of little value, because the needy lacked both the knowledge and the means to contribute.[8]

'Almost all the *disappointments*, *anxieties* and *vexations* of life,' Thompson concluded, were directly or indirectly attributable to the competitive system. There was:

no tranquillity, no peace of mind, no calm reliance on the certain effects of industry and integrity: all is a vortex of hope or apprehension. Truth and confidence between man and man form the exception not the rule to social intercourse. Rivalry and distrust, the necessary effects of competition, universally prevail. Among the fortunate, a universal fever of excitement not to increase enjoyment but to outrun each other burns through society. Among the poor rankle universal languor, depression, discontent and unhoping ignorance. Sometimes the glaring effects of insanity are produced, sometimes self-destruction, more often liability to disease and premature yielding to its ever ready attacks.[9]

And again:

Seldom can natural feelings display themselves – connections of what are called friendship and love are made with a view to wealth and domination. Envies, jealousies and hatreds are generated even after such connections are formed, or their formation is prevented by trifling differences of station. Despair and fury seize their victims. Melancholy or violence eat away the thread of existence. The mere animal part of sexual pleasure is bought by the richer of the dominant sex at the lowest price of competition and enjoyed as heartlessly and selfishly as any other purchased gratification. The weaker, poorer, selling parties when used are thrown by and trampled upon, generally to terminate life after a few years of feverish riot.[10]

These evils, social as well as economic, were inherent in the competitive system, and would last as long as the general interest was subordinated to private profit. Real progress could not be achieved until knowledge and beneficence replaced wealth as the object of human endeavour.

7

Population Theory

In Thompson's day the theories of Malthus exercised a powerful influence and cast a dark and forbidding shadow on every facet of social thought. The argument, which had been formulated to prove the impracticability of Godwinite communism, was that population, if otherwise unchecked, increased at a much faster rate than the means of subsistence; and that most proposals for social amelioration were useless if not injurious, misery and vice being necessary as 'preventive checks.' The pauper should be left to 'the punishment of nature, the punishment of severe want.' He had no right to breed, or to be bred, if the necessaries of life were lacking. A man born into a world already possessed had no claim of right to the smallest portion of food; he had in fact 'no business' to be alive: 'At Nature's mighty feast' there was 'no vacant cover for him'; she told him to be gone, and would 'quickly execute her own orders.'[1]

Unlike the orthodox economists, for whom this Malthusian theory was an essential article of faith, Thompson regarded its conclusions with aversion and dubbed it a 'great scarecrow' used 'to frighten away any attempt at social improvement.'[2] Yet, as an Irishman deeply concerned with a problem which was then more acute in his own country than anywhere else in the British Isles, he was at pains to make clear that he welcomed discussion on the population problem in so far as it tended to evolve a scientific outlook on the question. Together with Sismondi he was one of the very few opponents of Malthus ready to admit that the economists had presented a *prima facie* case worthy of consideration. Moreover, as a practical farmer, he criticized optimistic but woolly minded writers like the Co-operator Thomas Rowe Edmonds, who, in a work entitled *Practical, Moral and Political Economy*, claimed that the British Isles could feed 120 million people and six million horses. Thompson conceded that great improvements in agricultural technique might one day revolutionize the production of foodstuffs, but held that no one was justified 'in hazarding human happiness' on 'mere possibilities which might or might not be realized'; the population question would probably always remain 'one of the most important of the data on which calculations for human well-being must be founded.'[3]

Thompson followed Sismondi in rejecting the Malthusian argument that improvements in the condition of the people must be immediately negated by population increase, emphasizing that, on the contrary, the highest birthrate occurred where the people were most wretched, as in Ireland. Different standards of living in a single community also showed that the prosperity of the rich was not negated by limitless, 'improvident' breeding. Malthusian fears indeed were disproved by 'all the facts of history and all investigations of human motives.'[4] It was true that the tendency to multiply increased with the increase of comforts, but the tendency to improvident multiplication as certainly diminished. This awareness that population pressure was a problem of the 'poorest and most ignorant' communities, though an essential of population theory today, was an innovation in Thompson's day.[5]

Throughout his discussion he wrote with optimism concerning the future. He declared that though 'superstition and prejudices, the most grovelling and contemptible,' had hitherto 'usurped the place of reason and utility' in regulating the increase of the human race, knowledge was at last becoming triumphant and could no longer be 'proscribed by the dominant prevalence of a gloomy antipathy, wretched in itself and tormented by the aspect of the smiles and happiness of others.' Utility must be recognized as 'the only firm basis of morals.' It showed that rational man must limit his numbers in the same way as he prevented the overbreeding of sheep or silkworms, both of which possessed the same inherent capacity for increase as himself. It was absurd that he should regulate the increase of all other animals, while leaving to blind caprice his own increase, which was infinitely more important to him.[6]

Writing at a time when most of the ruling class were bitterly antagonistic to popular education and to ideas of population planning, Thompson remarked that the mass education necessary for a rational population policy was ruthlessly opposed by an upper class which realized that if the labourers bred less there would be less opportunity for exploitation. It was for this selfish reason that the privileged classes declared it 'absurd, wicked and impracticable' to educate the masses who were 'doomed for all eternity to labour, and nothing but labour.'

Thompson's advocacy of birth control which, like much of his thinking on population, may have been influenced by Sismondi, was altogether revolutionary for its time, and flew alike in the face of convention and ecclesiastical teaching. He openly declared that 'early marriages and universal healthiness' could coexist with a stationary population, and that sexual, intellectual, and moral pleasures might be much increased. Once it was recognized that 'the pleasures of casual intercourse could be enjoyed without any risk to population or any consequential evil to either party, the morality of utility and benevolence would look on such connections with more than an indulgent eye.'[7] This would be infinitely better than the existing state of affairs where sexual enjoyment had become 'a matter of trade like any other commodity,' being bought at the lowest possible price from the sex which had become 'the passive tool of male animal selfishness.'[8]

Existing marriage laws, Thompson argued, were the worst possible, being conclusive to 'blind animal increase.' Under existing laws a marriage, however reckless, could never be reversed or prevented from producing a large family tottering on the verge of starvation. 'With cold and cruel indifference' to the parties concerned and to the number of paupers propagated, a man and a woman were linked together for a lifetime 'with the alleged object of saving the children from destruction.' Rich males appropriated one portion of the females, those of their own class, for the purpose of propagation, while they purchased or meanly deceived the most beautiful of the women of the industrious classes for their more prized unconstrained enjoyments: 'Were the influential males really bound by the laws of marriage which they imposed on the females, the institution would not remain in its existing state another year.' With the emancipation of women the problem of population pressure would diminish, for whereas men enjoyed only the pleasures of union, women also encountered the pains, and might therefore be expected to show greater prudential foresight.[9]

Religious persons incapable of moral analysis and filled with 'nursery superstitions,' 'blind and undistinguishing moral dogmas' and 'early mental association of vice with freedom of sexual intercourse,' denounced 'in the gross, all sexual freedom,' failing to realize it would have been 'happy for the human race had the increase of numbers been left to individual regulation, protecting only the weak from the oppression of the strong,' instead of 'depriving one of the contracting parties of all rights, self-control and independence.'[10]

Such arguments aroused intense opposition, not only among the Irish Catholics who were Thompson's neighbours, but also in English society. George Jacob Holyoake records that fastidious friends of progress were not pleased that the prominent advocate of Co-operation was 'against large families.' The birth-control movement was at this time in its infancy, the *Inquiry* being perhaps the first important work to come out openly in its support.

8

Anna Wheeler and the Position of Women

In the early nineteenth century women of the labouring classes were drawn into the vortex of factory life in ever-increasing numbers, there to encounter the degradations of the new industrial civilization, the soul-destroying monotony of machine work, and long hours of toil under utterly wretched conditions. Neither the law nor the action of trade unions limited the hours of work, or compelled the fencing of dangerous machinery or the elimination of dangerous processes. Nevertheless, though the devices which enabled women of property to maintain a limited element of control over their possessions after marriage meant little to the women of the labouring classes, by escaping in some degree from the more solitary slavery of the home and by accepting the corporate bondage of factory life, working women were proving their usefulness and preparing the way for the development of a sense of independence.

Upper and middle-class women, on the other hand, found themselves confined in an age of transformation to lives of uselessness and frustration. Many of them had been brought up to live in accordance with the income and status of well-to-do husbands and fathers, but were left at their death in most meagre and even indigent circumstances owing to the custom of bequeathing the major share of the paternal fortune to the sons, leaving a bare pittance to the daughters and even to the widows. Women were rarely given an education which would enable them to enter the professions, and even had such education been granted almost all professions were closed to them. In consequence, it was widely assumed that they were innately less intelligent than men!

A married woman passed from the authority of her father to that of her husband, who acquired the right to her fidelity, her society, and her services. After marriage she possessed no legal personality, being under his direction, or, as it was termed, 'under coverture.' She could not sue or be sued in a Court of Law. She had no power to sign a deed or enter into a contract of any sort. She could not make a will without her husband's permission, which he could revoke at any time even after her death. She was entirely under his authority. She was obliged to live where he chose to reside; she had no right to bring her friends to his house without his permission or to object to anyone whom he might choose to introduce there. Any property she possessed at the time of her betrothal or inherited subsequently belonged to him, unless specially protected by a marriage settlement legally effected before the marriage. Such settlements were rare, and had the purpose not so much to enable a woman to have control over her own property as to guarantee to her father that his money should not be used to defray the expenses of an extravagant son-in-law. Even before marriage, from the time of her betrothal, a woman could not make a gift of anything belonging to her without her future husband's consent; to do so without his permission was to defraud him in the eyes of the law.[1]

A wife's earnings were the property of her husband, who could collect her wages from her employer or draw from the publisher the author's royalties on books she had written. Anything she purchased with her earnings belonged to him. The husband was entitled in his will to deprive his widow of all share in his personal property, including that which had been her own; she could only claim to remain forty days in his house, and that provided she did not re-marry.[2]

Children were the sole property of the father; at his death their guardianship and the power to direct their future passed to his nearest male relative. The man's authority over his children was an inalienable right, which he could in no way curtail by legal contract.

There was no divorce. The husband had the legal right to imprison his wife and to chastise her 'with a stick no thicker than his thumb'; in theory both parties had the right to apply to the Courts for an order enforcing 'the Restitution of Conjugal Rights'; but in practice this was only applied for the benefit of the husband. If a woman deserted her husband anyone who harboured her or assisted her in leaving his home could be sued by him. By deserting him she forfeited all claim to maintenance for herself and her children. But if she was the deserted party she had no power to obtain maintenance without proving her need in the Courts, and could not recover property which had belonged to her at the time of the marriage. Adultery on the part of the wife enabled the husband to obtain a judicial separation and terminated his legal responsibility to maintain her; infidelity on the part of her spouse, however, was not considered sufficient justification to enable her to withdraw her consortium.

The subjection of women, though generally regarded as entirely correct and normal in Thompson's time, had already been challenged by Mary Wollstonecraft from the women's point of view, by Godwin, Saint-Simon, and Owen from the Socialist standpoint, and by Jeremy Bentham from that of the Utilitarians. Thompson, for his part, considered that championship of the emancipation of women was basically interrelated to opposition to private property, the State, and organized religion. In his eyes the existing system was the perpetuation of a barbarous age. Men acted not in accordance with reason, but under the domination of false passions, restraints, and animosities imposed on them by their environment. They were poisoned by the system of private property, which caused them to act not in accordance with enlightened social interest but with the 'supposed' interest of each against all. They found themselves divided into warring factions, filled with anti-social passions, and openly proclaiming an antagonistic and competitive philosophy. The State, the only institution with any claim to direct social policy, was nothing more than the instrument by which one class waged war on its opponents. Marriage was the legalized prostitution by which man seized upon woman for his pleasure, taking advantage of her dependence to force her into virtual slavery. Religion was bogus – trickery by which the clergy obtained a life of idleness in return for doling out supernatural sanction to whomsoever feared the advance of reason might challenge their privileges. By its means education was held in fetters, the rich staved off the clamour of the poor, and marriage and other institutions were shrouded in superstition and proclaimed 'sacred.'

Blending a Saint-Simonian contempt for the past with a Benthamite ideal for the future, Thompson contended that to have expected 'absolute wisdom' to spring up amid 'feudal proscription of intellect' was as absurd as 'to expect that the steamship would have sprung forth as soon as the first boat of wickerwork and skins was launched on the waves.' Nevertheless, with the advance of reason, man was destined to escape from the tyranny forced upon him by history. He would mould his own life by recasting his environment. To do so the traditional institutions of society must all be transformed; they could not be accepted by rational man merely because they had been bequeathed to him by the age of barbarism.[3] Marriage and the family, private property, religion, and the State must all be recast. Women would be raised to equality with men, and marriage laws would become 'perfectly equal between the two sexes,' allowing dissolution at the wish of either party, appropriate regulations being provided for the protection of mother and children. The propagation of the species would then become the responsibility of the community; 'women would have no inducement to subject themselves to the irrevocable despotism of marriage laws, thereby yielding up their independence for food, or for a shortlived and artificially magnified gratification.' Every community would devise regulations for the intercourse of men and women:

> based entirely on principles of utility and enlightened reason, having happiness solely in view, instead of the caprice or ascetism adopted by the different sects without the remotest concern for the miseries or happiness produced by them, forbidding all inquiry because incapable of affording reasons.

Intercourse outside marriage would be accepted whenever it did not entail an imprudent increase in numbers.

> All intercourse tending to happiness or a preponderance of good over evil might then be termed 'marriage' to gratify those who have been accustomed to associate morals with the letters forming certain mystic words or with certain arbitrary and entirely unessential ceremonies.'[4]

Thompson's championship of women's emancipation was undoubtedly intensified by his close friend and collaborator, Anna Wheeler, whose forceful personality and bitter experiences added poignancy and emphasis to his writings.

Anna Wheeler, who was born in 1785, was the youngest daughter of the famous Irish Protestant divine, Archbishop Doyle. Her childhood was spent in rural Ireland, where she became 'the reigning beauty' of the countryside. She married at the early age of fifteen. Her husband, Francis Massy Wheeler, a grandson of the second Lord Massy, was a mere youth of nineteen and a spoilt only child. On the death of his parents three years earlier he had succeeded to the family estate of Ballywire at Lizard Connell in County Limerick. He had conceived a passion for Anna Doyle on seeing her at the races. The widowed Mrs Doyle had been strongly opposed to young Massy's advances. She had persuaded her brother-in-law, General Sir John Doyle, to invite Anna and her sister Bessie to visit him in London, but the diversion failed to effect its purpose; the marriage was soon announced. The mind of the young wife was deeply alive to social interests and to nascent ideas of progress. She was proud that Henry Grattan, the famous Irish patriot, was her godfather. Her marriage was to prove a disastrous failure. Massy Wheeler was a dipsomaniac and degenerating rapidly. Their home in the long grey house at Ballywire was falling into decay. The leaking roof was unrepaired, the drive unweeded, the boundary walls disintegrating. The master of the house spent half his days lounging in the stables or on horseback and every evening drank himself into a stupor.[5]

It was a tragic home for a youthful bride reared in an atmosphere of refinement and mental activity. Within twelve years she had borne half a dozen children all of whom, save two girls, Henrietta and Rosina, died in their tender infancy.

Nevertheless, endowed with remarkable tenacity and strength of character, she persevered with a systematic study of social and political philosophy, obtaining by post from London the works of the foremost exponents of egalitarian democracy, among them the still heatedly debated writings of the pioneer feminist revolutionary, Mary Wollstonecraft.

Local opinion commiserated Massy Wheeler on account of his wife's absorption in study, for despite his own alcoholic failing it was held that her duty as a married woman was to immerse herself wholly in the interests of her spouse.

Writing in after years, Mrs Wheeler's younger daughter, Rosina, while complaining that the influence of Mary Wollstonecraft's writings had warped her mother's judgment, nevertheless with scathing sarcasm declared that though her mother's family had been renowned since the days of Edward III for their wit and the brilliancy of their attainments, her paternal ancestors had been 'Titled Fools' at the conquest and had 'continued uninterrupted so without the plebeian taint of brains having come between them and their nobility.' She remembered her mother 'stretched on a sofa, deep in the perusal of some French or German philosophical work that had reached her via London.'

A letter from Anna Wheeler to Robert Owen reveals that the voluminous reading for which she was often censured included *The System of Nature*, by the rationalists Holbach and Diderot. She considered it revealed that mankind had 'hitherto been taught nothing but the most pernicious errors'; the 'moral degradation and deplorable wretchedness' of the race could not, however, be removed, except by slow degrees and 'bit by bit reforms'; the public seemed to prefer 'to endure all that sensation can endure rather than have its sores treated.' She complained that the doctrines of Christ, 'our Eastern philosopher' as she terms him, were always used as 'zealous and blind advocates of a mischievous dogma for some narrow end.' She dismissed patriotism as 'an ignorant mother whose partiality strained heaven and earth for one child which in her blindness loaded she with a thousand evils.' Society, she concluded, considered women should have no feelings of any kind but should 'pretend to an overwhelming degree of admiration for their respective masters, whether wise or foolish, cruel or kind.' As long as men remained content with themselves and their barbarous practices, those most interested (their wives) must not tell them they were wrong, nor must they be able to discern good from evil. '"Shall man be free and woman a slave," and idiot? says Shelley – never say I!'[6]

The break-up of the Wheeler household took place as soon as the wife became sufficiently free of childbearing to make her escape. In August 1812 she fled with her children to Sir John Doyle, then Governor of Guernsey. Massy Wheeler refused to make any allowance toward the support of his wife and daughters; nevertheless, correspondence continued with him until his death in 1820.

In the splendid setting of Guernsey Government House, the Governor's vivacious and talented niece became a prominent social figure. She was in her element in a cosmopolitan society, and so greatly impressed the old Duc de Bouillon, a cousin of the future King Charles X of France, that he became for twelve years her suitor, addressing her in madrigals and epigrams. Rosina described her mother at this period as very tall with an exceedingly white skin delicately flushed with rose, a high forehead surmounted by rippling dark chestnut hair, deep greyblue eyes with dark lashes and eyebrows, a delicately chiselled aquiline nose, and short curling upper lip. Her mouth 'the most beautiful I ever saw with teeth dazzling as a row of oriental pearls'; her smile 'the most enchanting and the most excellent thing in women, a low sweet voice.'

At the end of 1816, when Mrs Wheeler left Guernsey, almost the whole population assembled to bid her farewell; she sailed to London, where she met Henry Grattan before paying a short visit to Dublin. A little later she found her way to Caen, where she became the centre of a Saint-Simonian circle, by whom she was hailed as the 'Goddess of Reason' and 'the most gifted woman of the age.' In the early 'twenties she met Charles Fourier only recently arrived in Paris and still unknown. The French Socialist, who had sent extracts of his works to Prime Minister Villèle and others without arousing any interest, was greatly cheered when she expressed strong support for his ideas. It was agreed that he should consult Robert Owen, and a meeting was actually arranged in August, though the two Socialists did not join forces. Towards the close of 1823 or early in 1824 Anna Wheeler returned to London, where she was in close contact with Bentham. She was soon also a frequent visitor at Woodcot, the house of the novelist Bulwer Lytton, who married her daughter Rosina in August 1827, despite the protests of his mother, Mrs Wheeler's revolutionary ideas being repugnant to her.

Anna Wheeler became widely known in the metropolis, where she took an important place in the Co-operative, Feminist, and Saint-Simonian circles. Disraeli described her as 'something between Jeremy Bentham and Meg Merrilies, very clever, but awfully revolutionary.' George Jacob Holyoake records that she was a frequent writer in Co-operative periodicals and delivered 'well-reasoned' lectures which 'attracted considerable attention.' She urged women 'not to leave the bitter inheritance of ignorance and slavery' to their daughters; throughout the social fabric, she protested, were 'vice, crime and dissocial anarchy'; happiness was 'lost to all' because security was 'unknown to any.' Were she to die without a sign expressive of her 'horror, indignation, and bitter contempt' for the 'masked barbarism' of 'so-called civilized society' her regret at having lived only to serve and suffer in the capacity of 'slave and woman' would be complete.

All this time she was in close contact with Owen, who invariably sent her copies of his published writings. She reciprocated by advising him on developments in French progressive movements; she conveyed to him a report that the partisans of Fourier would be 'the very first' to rally to his banner; that he would be surrounded by 'a strong and enlightened party' and that 'no obstacle' was to be feared from the French Government. She was in France when he arrived and introduced him to Flora Tristan and many other advanced thinkers. Her fervour for the French Revolution of 1830 caused the Fourierist, Hugh Doherty, to send her a knot of tricolour taken from the barricades, and to express the wish that she would return to Paris, where 'the rights of women are constantly put forth in all the clubs though not as yet in the public press.' She was also in close contact with the Saint-Simonians, and served as a link beteen them and the English Socialist movement, translating extracts from their writings for the English Co-operative press.[7]

The names of William Thompson and Anna Wheeler are often linked in the records of the Co-operative Movement. Theirs was a friendship of mutual opinions and ideals unique in its day, for the rigid conventions of the time and the immense disparity between the educations afforded to the sexes made intellectual contact between men and women extremely rare. In many ways their friendship is strikingly reminiscent of that of John Stuart Mill and Harriet Taylor, which even a generation later contrasted strangely with the customs of the day. Anna Wheeler and Harriet Taylor, it is interesting to note, were both women of intense personality, socialistically inclined and keen advocates of the rights of women.

William Thompson and Anna Wheeler discussed together most aspects of the 'social question' and, above all, the subjection and degradation of women. The fruit of this collaboration was Thompson's *Appeal of One Half the Human Race*,[8] which is dedicated to his fair compatriot and has her portrait as a frontispiece. The Dutch banker, H. P. G. Quack, picturesquely writes 'On opening Thompson's old book the nobility of Anna Wheeler's figure and the sweetness of her expression stand out like a pressed flower discovered anew.' In his dedication Thompson declares that part of his book was the exclusive product of 'her mind and pen'; the remainder was their 'joint property,' he being her 'scribe and interpreter' who had endeavoured to express feelings which 'emanated' from her mind. Though he himself had long reflected on them, she had actually suffered from 'the inequalities of sexual laws'; he was therefore indebted to her for 'those bolder and more comprehensive views, which perhaps can only be elicited by the concentration of the mind on one darling though terrific theme.'

He declared he had long hesitated to publish their common ideas in the hope that she would herself take up the cause of her sex, and give to the world what she had so often stated in her conversation 'and under feigned names in such of the periodical publications of the day as would tolerate such a theme.' A woman's hand would then have had 'the honour of raising from the dust the neglected banner' which thirty years earlier Mary Wollstonecraft's *Vindication of the Rights of Woman* had 'boldly unfolded in the face of the prejudices of thousands of years.' Despite his eulogy, Thompson regarded the views expressed in this historic work as 'too narrow'; Anna Wheeler's, on the contrary, were 'totally free of prejudice'; 'her eye was open to the rays of truth from whatever quarter they might emanate,' and the only reason why he and not she had written the *Appeal* was that 'for her, leisure, and resolution to undertake the drudgery of the task were wanting.'

Thompson and his vivacious compatriot had many ideas in common. Both were bitter opponents of marriage, its then unbreakable bonds, the disabilities it imposed upon women, and the flagrantly unequal moral standard to which it imparted a false odour of sanctity. Both were ardent pioneers of the pristine Co-operative Movement and had emerged into the sphere of propaganda after considerable study. Anna Wheeler's advanced views thus contrasted greatly with the timid attitude of the women propagandists who half a century later confined their advocacy to one or other aspect of the women's cause, venturing only to plead for a limited parliamentary franchise, fearing even to hint at the possibility that women might be elected to the legislature. The deep unity of thought between her and Thompson may be deduced from his dedication:

> You look forward, as do I, to a state of society very different from that which now exists, in which the effort of all is to outwit, supplant and snatch from each other; where interest is systematically opposed to duty, where the so-called system of morals is little more than a mass of hypocrisy preached by knaves but unpractised by them, to keep their slaves, male as well as female, in blind uninquiring obedience; and where the whole motley fabric is kept together by fear and blood. You look forward to a better state of society, where the principle of benevolence shall supersede that of fear; where restless and anxious individual competition shall give place to mutual co-operation and joint possession; where individuals, in large numbers male and female, forming voluntary associations, shall become a mutual guarantee to each other for the supply of all useful wants, and form an unsalaried insurance company where perfect freedom of opinion and perfect equality will reign, and where the children of all will be equally educated and provided for by the whole.

He declared he could hear Anna Wheeler 'indignantly reject the boon of equality with such creatures as men now are'; really enlightened women, 'disdaining the submissive tricks of the slave and the caprices of the despot,' found it difficult to find associates among men who claimed respect 'only from the strength of their arm and the lordly faculty of producing beards attached to their chins'; Co-operation would, however, elevate both sexes; but to achieve full equality every facet of irrationality and hypocrisy would have to be ruthlessly challenged: 'We laugh at the Chinese for abridging the useful and hence beautiful form of women's feet by compression to the standard of five or six inches in length, but from exactly the same love of vain distinction we deform and compress the waist of women of our rich class to the diameter of a few inches.[9]

9

The *Appeal*: A Reply to James Mill

Though opposition to the disabilities and unequal status of women was theoretically common ground for the followers of Godwin, Bentham, and Saint-Simon, there was a tendency for the more respectable Utilitarians to compromise; some feared to incur personal opprobrium; others believed that to espouse the women's cause was to endanger other reforms.

Thompson and Anna Wheeler were gravely concerned about the 'backsliding' of thinkers whose principles ought to have made them unswerving champions of the women's cause. As Bentham's personal friends, nurtured in Utilitarian thought, they were outraged when Pierre Etienne Dumont of Geneva, one of Bentham's chief popularizers, publicly announced his opposition to women's suffrage. This action, by a writer often regarded as Bentham's official spokesman, appeared even more alarming when Dumont was joined by no less a figure than James Mill, who, among the Utilitarians, was second only to Bentham himself. In his celebrated *Article on Government*, which he wrote in 1820 for the 1824 supplement to the *Encyclopaedia Britannica*, Mill declared it 'pretty clear' that all individuals whose interests were 'indisputably included' in those of other individuals could be denied political representation 'without inconvenience.' In this category he included not only children but also women, on the ground that the interest of almost all of them was 'involved in that of their fathers or that of their husbands.' These words, which produced heated controversy among the more progressive Utilitarians, profoundly shocked every supporter of the emancipation of women. Their author's own son, John Stuart Mill, and the majority of his friends 'most positively dissented' from his father's position, and Bentham himself remonstrated; but all in vain. The elder Mill gave instructions in 1825 for his *Article* to be reissued in pamphlet form without amendment.

Thompson declared that he and Anna Wheeler continued expecting that a well-known public figure would issue a refutation. They had 'looked upon every day as the last' before 'the rude gauntlet thrown down against half mankind would be snatched up' to arrest the 'inroad of barbarism into the nineteenth century' which Mill had made 'under the guise of philosophy.' But as no answer appeared, he felt himself obliged to reply, and did so in his 234-page *Appeal of One Half the Human Race*. This book, which appeared in 1825, was in fact the sole public protest against the *Article*, though four years later its reissue in Mill's *Collected Works* called forth a strong disclaimer from the future Lord Macaulay in the *Edinburgh Review*.

What Thompson particularly objected to about Mill's attack was that it was not the work of 'the vulgar hirelings or everyday bigots of existing institutions,' but was 'put forward under the shield of philosophy preached by the preachers of Utility.' Mill was entitled to respect for his championship of the political rights of men, but it was strange that a philosopher and a lover of wisdom who avowedly sought the greatest possible quantity of human happiness, should 'deliberately, in the very threshold of his argument, put aside *one-half* the human race, of all ages, and all characters and conditions, as unentitled to consideration.' Were his philosophy founded on the assumption that man was necessarily a beneficent being, the inference that power over women might safely be placed in his hands would 'at least be fairly drawn from the premises.' In reality, however, the whole fabric of his thought held that men necessarily abused their power over others, that this tendency, where unrestrained, would reduce the victims to the condition of West Indian slaves. When he referred to women's interests being included in those of men he was thus abandoning his own 'grand governing law of human nature.' Such an exception, embracing half the human race, was 'a pretty large exception' requiring 'all the boldness of an English philosopher' to sustain it. For, on the assumption that all women are justly ruled by men, if one man could be found treating justly a fellow man over whom he had power, arguments for self-government would logically have to be replaced by the postulate that arbitrary power is in a majority of cases beneficial.

Thompson argued, however, that Mill had clarified the issue in as far as he had abandoned the old arguments against the enfranchisement of women. There was no more pretence that they were 'incapable of becoming rational,' that they were too weak or too prone to incapacity on account of childbearing. There were no more suggestions that the vote was undesirable because the sexes should be kept different or because the existing order might be overthrown. Nor was it still claimed that men were the stronger half of the species, and therefore entitled to render women, like any other objects of desire, tributary of their enjoyment. Mill had not even suggested that the attempt of men to obtain a wider suffrage might be endangered. Instead, his 'more refined sophistry' had staked the whole of his case on a new invention – the argument of 'included interests.' It was significant of Mill's attitude to women, however, that he coupled them with children, and only allocated them a bare six lines in his thirty-two pages on the principles of government! In the case of children society had discovered that identity of interests was a 'fiction,' and had come to recognize the need for regulations to protect them from the abuse of their parents. Children, in fact, were excluded from politics, not because their interests were 'included' in those of their parents, but because their bodily and mental powers were not fully developed. This argument was palpably not applicable to women, and it was for that reason that the Utilitarian philosopher had invented his fiction of 'identity of interests.'

Between a fourth and a sixth of the whole adult population was composed of women who possessed neither husband nor father. The logical deduction from James Mill's contention was that, like men, they were entitled to political rights, indeed the fact that they were denied all opportunities of education and were physically weaker than men gave them even greater need of representation. Yet this important exception to the rule had been totally ignored in the hasty generalizations of the *Article on Government*! If Mill, the philosopher and moralist, had been arrested by the police in the company of a dozen smugglers, and it was decided by a jury that nearly all the thirteen were guilty and that they should therefore all be transported, the innocent Mill would have received exactly the same treatment he had afforded to these women.

Adult daughters who remained in their parents' household similarly failed to fit into Mill's theory, for though denied political representation, they enjoyed some rights in law. Their interests were, if anything, more akin to those of their mothers than to those of their lordly fathers, who deigned but rarely or through condescension to interest themselves in 'the little pleasures of their daughters, the colours and fashions of their clothes' and the other matters left to them as 'suited to their amiable imbecility.' Men trained their daughters 'to look out of their artificial cages of restraint and imbecility' to catch glances of an outside world which they would only attain by leaving behind them the very names of their fathers, 'vainly hoping for independence in the gratification of one passion, love, round which their absurd training for blind male sensuality had caused all their little anxieties to centre.' Their brothers, on the other hand, who shared the occupations and pleasures of their fathers, had been accorded the franchise, though it might have been contended that their interests were already covered by the paternal vote. There was therefore no logical case for the exclusion of daughters.

Thompson became deeply impassioned when he turned to the oppressed status of the married woman, whom he described as 'an involuntary breeding machine and household slave.' He complained that historically men had always used their skill and cunning to render their fellow beings subservient to them; women on account of their weakness had been the easiest to subjugate, and had been parcelled out for the 'sexual delights of their masters,' their minds and habits being 'moulded to the barbarous supposed interests of their short-sighted keepers.' If the fair sex had not pleased men sexually they would have been relegated to the position of a subject tribe of manual workers for the exclusive benefit of the males.[1] He arraigned the marriage contract in scathing and indignant terms:

Each man yokes a woman to his establishment, and calls it a *contract*. Audacious falsehood! Where are any of the attributes of contracts, of equal and just contracts? A contract implies the voluntary assent of both the contracting parties. Can even both the parties by agreement alter the terms, as to *indissolubility*[2] and inequality? No. Can any individual man divest himself, were he even so inclined, of his power of despotic control? He cannot. Have women been consulted as to the terms of this pretended contract all of whose enjoyments are on one side, while all its pains and privations are on the other – a contract giving all power, arbitrary will and unbridled enjoyment to the one side; to the other, unqualified obedience, and enjoyments meted out or withheld at the caprice of the ruling and enjoying party?[3]

The argument that women had freedom of choice as to whether they would marry or not was invalid, for the prevailing customs denied them an independent livelihood; the great majority had to marry 'on whatever terms their masters willed, or starve; or if not absolutely starve, they must renounce at least all the means of enjoyment monopolized by the males.' Husbands and wives were not equally dependent on each other; public opinion allowed a man to gratify every sexual desire outside legal wedlock, while women were only allowed to satisfy their desires within the marriage bond. If a wife did not comply with the caprices of her husband he was permitted 'by vile law, and viler opinion, to compel obedience,'[4] though if he refused any request of hers he was the sole arbiter. By accepting this state of affairs man had surrendered 'the delights of equality, esteem and friendship,' and his pride and selfishness had been magnified to fantastic proportions.

The touchstone to test the 'identity of interests' between husband and wife was whether they enjoyed equal pleasures. An examination of the facts revealed that in respect of the sensual pleasures, eating and drinking, man had weighted the scales to his own advantage; he had made himself the ruler of the household and the controller of the purse; he denied a woman education and forbade her the right to make friendships at will. The infidelity of the husband, though necessarily involving the happiness of the wife, met with no redress; while the infidelity of his spouse, which would scarcely detract from his happiness, was 'revenged with a complication of punishments greater than those accorded by law to many of the most atrocious crimes.' Without legal, moral, or physical power to restrain him, the wife was 'compelled silently to witness whatever extravagances of unbridled libertinism the husband might think proper to indulge in,' smothering her repinings, 'happy if she escaped the further consequential evils of violence and disease, the natural attendants of his misgoverned passions.' Home, except on a few occasions 'chiefly for the drillings of superstition to render her obedience more submissive,' was 'the eternal prison-house of the wife'; her husband painted it as the abode of calm bliss, but took care 'to find outside its doors a species of bliss not quite so calm, but of a more varied and stimulating description.'[5] Though the law might give a wife some protection against strangers, she was given none against her husband 'to whose restraints and wrongs all her actions, words and thoughts' were ceaselessly exposed. Her only possibility of redress was in the case of starvation or violence endangering her life, both of which accusations were difficult for her to prove; any complaints on her part would be easily avenged by the domestic despot to whom she was united by an indissoluble bond.[6] She had been expected to swear obedience at the time of her marriage, yet on the death of the husband she lost the breadwinner and had no legal claim to her deceased husband's property, not even to her former possessions, which had become his as a result of the marriage. Yet Mill had dared to write of an 'inclusion of interests!'

It was impossible under any circumstances for 'the happiness of any individual to be included in that of another.' The ox was better fed when the master was rich, but the common interest existed merely because it was in the interest of the master that the ox should be fattened as speedily as possible in order to be consumed! The very act of making one person dependent on another would destroy such 'identity of interests' as might exist; the development of the individual would also be frustrated, for acts, however beneficial in themselves, lacked moral value if performed under compulsion. The mere fact that men clung to their power over women was a demonstration that in their opinion there were necessarily occasions when the interests of the two parties differed. Although enlightened men recognized the wisdom of not enforcing the marriage bond to the full, society, by retaining it, ignored that it was employed 'not by the wise for good objects, but by the ignorant and brutal for bad purposes.'[7]

Having offered proof that the interests of women were not 'included' in those of men, Thompson proceeded to argue that even if 'inclusion' existed it could never justify a denial of civil and political rights. Women were 'one half the human race' and as much entitled to happiness as men. The happiness of society could not be attained without making all its members happy, and to use such phrases as 'the public good' in any other sense was mere metaphysics and 'mountebank jargon.' Though political rights were usually demanded on the score that without them men had never enjoyed civil rights, they were also required for the beneficial effect they had on the individual; they led his attention from himself to matters in which large numbers of his fellow creatures were interested.[8] In considering the status of half the human race Mill had overlooked this. He had not seen that the need for self-realization entirely invalidated the relevance of the claim of 'inclusion of interests.' It was not enough to ensure that the material interests of women should be cared for by men, even had they done it efficiently; self-realization could not be achieved as mere passive subjects of administration, but only as active agents creating the well-being of the community. Wherever people were denied a share in government misery and oppression reigned unchecked.

Finally, even if it were assumed that the interests of one sex were 'included' in that of the other, could anyone deny that the vote would be a most innocent and useful pleasure to women? What harm could it do? Who could benefit by depriving them if interests were identical and man's monopolization of the suffrage was not 'an engine of ulterior oppression'?[9]

In fact, however, civil rights were impossible without political representation. The subordinate political status of women had a profound effect on public opinion and served as an excuse for the more tyrannical men to practise the 'old domestic atrocities of despotism' which public opinion was beginning to condemn, though still allowed by the law. Few could be consistently good all their lives; therefore the law should not sanction bad behaviour, the more so as it was hard for the holder of despotic power to judge impartially in his own case. If men desired to give women equality in other matters, why did they refuse it in the political sphere? Did men maintain 'the exclusive power of making unequal laws with the sincere wish of making none but those which are equal?' That this was not the case was evident since the very men who excluded women also excluded other men.[10] How could legislators know the interests of women, whom they never consulted and who had no control over them, being even debarred from expressing their opinions by 'the insolent and stultifying custom' which prevented them addressing meetings.[11] In the case of men, with all their superior opportunities of influence, it had been everywhere found that where political rights were denied equal civil and criminal laws were not forthcoming. It was therefore clear that equality for women could only be achieved if there were political rights to enforce it; this meant there must be women voters and women members of Parliament, women judges and women jurors. Utilitarians like James Mill should realize these facts. Unless they gave up applying their principles as though they wished to promote the happiness of men alone, 'Utility' would become a purely cabalistic term like 'Church' and 'State,' and the whole basis of their philosophy would collapse.

Besides replying to James Mill, the *Appeal* contained a lengthy exposition of the views of Thompson and Anna Wheeler couched in forceful and often extremely passionate language. The author referred with sarcasm to those who denied women the vote on account of their weakness: if strength were the qualification, why was the franchise not based on a weight-lifting contest and why was the claim of the elephant denied? It was contemptible for men to argue that they alone should have the vote because women were incapacitated by pregnancy and the rearing of children. Men scorned women's period of gestation, yet they expected commiseration when they were themselves for any reason incapacitated! Thompson uttered a bitter condemnation of these arguments:

> Shameless slanderers as ye are! Heartless hypocrites! Look to your legislative, your *representative*, assembly, as ye term it, your six hundred and fifty-eight *men*, night after night, dismissed because forty are not present, occupied in all the rounds of sensuality and other vices, preying upon the very women whom ye slander, and then, if the network between the terminations of your arteries and veins has not become impervious to indignant blood, blush – if ye can blush where women are concerned – blush for your impotent ridicule, for your affectation of mischief arising from such a cause.[12]

There was no evidence that either sex was inherently superior. It should not be forgotten, however, that women as the weaker party were most in need of protection. Moreover, as mothers, they would be 'equally interested in promoting the happiness of their sons as of their daughters.' Though as yet they lacked specialized knowledge, they were by no means deficient in general knowledge and wisdom, which was the main requirement in a legislator. By bringing probity into public life, by practising the arts of persuasion and peace and by avoiding offensive wars which were the scourge of humanity, women would be assisting human life to 'transform itself into a paradise.' Legislation required the nurse, rather than the warrior, 'not activity which would lift much, run much, or slay much, but which would watch much, and with never ceasing patience, endure much.'

The emancipation of the subject sex would be accompanied by intense excitement on the part of women and alarm among conservative and timid men. Women would soon enter most of the professions, though it would be a long time before they obtained full equality with men. There should, however, be no suggestion of taking the produce of the strong man for the benefit of the weak woman, as that would endanger incentive. All that women required was the removal of political and social discriminations and the right to compete with men on equal terms. They asked for the same opportunities for education as men, the same chance to enter the professions, and the same political, civil, and domestic rights. They demanded an equal system of morals in which 'the same action attended by the same consequences, whether committed by man or woman, should be attended with the same approbation or disapprobation.'[13]

Like the Saint-Simonians, Thompson was profoundly convinced that the emancipation of women and the transformation of the economic system were closely interrelated. He declared that complete social liberation was impossible for either sex as long as the competitive system remained. Under Co-operation, as envisaged by Owen and Fourier, women would no longer be forced to sell the use of their person or suffer economic privation as a result of the desertion or loss of the breadwinner; they would be freed from the drudgery of the house and the ceaseless attendance on young children.[14]

Though nothing short of Co-operation would entirely heal the 'flagrant evils of the social system,' the mere removal of the legal disabilities of women would lead to a 'wonderful improvement' in the human race. The vote would be an 'invigorating charm that would lead out the minds of women from an eternal association with mere childhood and childish toys' and elevate them 'from isolation and stupidity to high intercourse with the minds of men equally cultivated and beneficent with their own.'

The appeal must therefore go out to generous people of both sexes. To men:

> Be consistent, men! Ye stronger half of the race, be at length rational! Three or four thousand years have worn threadbare your vile cloak of hypocrisy. Even women, your poor, weak, contented slaves, at whose impotence of penetration, the result of your vile exclusions, you have been accustomed to laugh, begin to see through it and to shudder at the loathsomeness beneath. Cast aside this tattered cloak before it leaves you naked and exposed. Clothe yourselves with new garments of sincerity. Be rational human beings, not mere male sexual creatures ...

Women, too, must be active in their own liberation, for freedom is never received 'as a gift from the masters':

> Women of England, women, in whatever country ye breathe – wherever ye breathe degraded – awake! Awake to the contemplation of the happiness that awaits you when all your faculties of mind and body shall be fully cultivated and developed; when every path in which ye can exercise those improved faculties shall be laid open and rendered delightful to you, even as to them who now ignorantly enslave and degrade you ... The unvaried despotism of so many

thousand years has not entirely degraded you. .... Do no blushes rise among you – swells no breast with indignation at the enormous wrong. Simple as ye are, have ye become enamoured of folly? ... Do ye pretend to enjoy with him, at this banquet of *bought* or *commanded* sensuality, the sensuality of prostitution or of marriage? ... of dependence on man, gratifying by one operation his two ruling animal propensities, sexual desire and love of dominion.

Whatever pleasures you enjoy are permitted you for man's sake; nothing is your own; possession of person and of property are alike withheld from you. Nothing is yours but secret pangs, the bitter burning tears of regret, the stifled sobs of outraged nature, thrown back upon your own hearts where the vital principle itself stands checked or is agitated by malignant passions until body and mind become the frequent prey to overwhelming disease, now finding vent in sudden frenzy, now plunged in pining melancholy, or bursting the weak tenement of reason, seeking relief in self-destruction.

How many thousands of your sex perish daily unpitied and unknown, often the victims of pressing want, always of privation and the arbitrary laws of heartless custom, condemned to cheerless solitude, or an idiot round of idle fashionable pursuits! Your morning of life perhaps passed by and with it the lingering, darling hope of sympathy expired; you were puppets once of doting, ignorant parents, whose tenderness for you outlived not your first youth. Careless of your future fate, they 'launched you into life without an oar,' indigent and ignorant, to eat the tear-steeped bread of dependence, as wives, sisters, hired mistresses, or unpitied prostitutes! This is the fate of many, nay, of all your sex, subject only to those shades of difference arising from the very peculiar circumstances of the accident of independent fortune. The general want of knowledge, which is withheld from your sex, keeps even those individuals who are favoured by fortune bowed to the relentless yoke which man's laws, his superstitions and hypocritical morality, have prepared for you.

Thus degraded to the level of mere automatons, the passive tools of the pleasures and passions of men, your actions are regulated, like those of slaves, by the arbitrary will of masters, to whom, by the necessities of existence uniting yourselves, you are compelled to vow uninquiring obedience. O wretched slaves of such wretched masters! Awake, arise, shake off these fetters.[15]

Thompson planned to follow up the *Appeal* with a comparative survey of the position of married women in different countries which would illustrate his belief that the happiness of a community varied with the degree of equality between husbands and wives, a theory which he may have derived from Fourier, who had contended that the extension of the rights of women was 'the general principle of social progress.' The many and varied activities which the Irish Socialist crowded into the last eight years of his life prevented him from completing this survey, though he continued his powerful advocacy of the women's cause through the Press and on the platform. In an *Address to Mechanics*, which appeared in 1826, he declared that as long as women were left uneducated men would find truly cultured home life impossible and, however acquainted with the sciences they might be, would remain 'no better than the lordly owners of West India or Virginia slaves.'[16] In another article he argued that the improvement of the human race, like that of other animals discussed by the French evolutionist, Lamarck, depended on the development of both sexes. The education of women was the most important, because the mother played a larger role than the father in developing the faculties of the child. Intellectual and moral progress, however, required the cultivation of both parents; hitherto the failure to educate half the race had led to 'an internecine war of light and darkness' between the sexes, every improvement in the males being 'counteracted and reduced by the opposing interests of the neglected and absurdly despised females.' When man came to perceive the 'frightful chasm' he had made in his happiness by rendering himself 'the despot instead of the friend and equal' of the other half of his race, he would realize that family despotism was 'artificially trained' and that the mistake of condoning it as 'human nature' was one of the most serious factors retarding human improvement.[17]

This propaganda of William Thompson and Anna Wheeler is important in the history of the emancipation of women as well as in that of Socialist thought. The *Appeal* was the first voice of a nineteenth-century man against the degradation of women and the first piece of literature written with a direct bearing on suffrage legislation. It was in fact the most significant work in the seventy odd years between the publication of Mary Wollstonecraft's *Vindication of the Rights of Women* of 1792 and John Stuart Mill's *Subjection of Women* in 1869. Like the rest of Thompson's works, it was too startling to be reviewed in the orthodox Press, but received a cordial reception in Socialist and Co-operative circles which, like the Saint-Simonian movement in

France, were favourably disposed towards the strange new idea of the emancipation of women. Thompson must have been well known to many prominent Utilitarians on account of his residence with Bentham, and it is therefore unlikely that his reply to so important a Utilitarian as James Mill was unread by them. A translation of at least part of Thompson's book appears to have been published in France, perhaps by the Saint-Simonians, for Alexander Walker, in a widely read work of 1833, reproduces a passage in French in which the Irish Socialist attacks the 'hypocritical and unequal nature' of marriage and sex morality.[18] Thompson's ideas were also not unknown in the United States, where his address to Anna Wheeler was included in a popular social anthology entitled *The Bible of Nature*, edited and published by George Henry Evans, the American Radical and founder of the *Working Man's Advocate*. It is broadly true to say that Co-operators and Socialists generally accepted the emancipation of women as an integral part of the Co-operative ideal. In 1840 J. Phillips, a Co-operator of Hyde in Cheshire, declared that under Co-operation 'females will have their proper station in society, when they will no longer be considered the playthings and slaves of men,' while the *Communist Manifesto* of Marx and Engels declared in 1848 that the bourgeois 'never dreams for a moment that our main purpose is to ensure that women shall no longer occupy the position of mere instruments of production.'

The propaganda of William Thompson and Anna Wheeler, and of the Co-operators and Communists who followed them, is therefore of vital relevance to the history of ideas regarding the emancipation of women. Before the *Appeal*, and even anterior to Mary Wollstonecraft's *Vindication of the Rights of Women*, there had been stirrings of discontent among women and restless desires for wider freedoms and opportunities. But they had been of a tentative, vague, and often timid character; no clear programme of reform had been enunciated. Thompson's book gave a more concrete and comprehensive view of the legal and social disabilities of women; it adopted an altogether bolder and more challenging approach than had yet been attempted, and gave point and impetus to latent yearnings. From its time onward publications advocating the emancipation of women became more frequent, bolder, and more definitely applied to remedy the evils of the law. True, many who were roused to activity in the cause of women's emancipation by this forceful work failed to agree with the whole of its philosophy. Many failed to follow its Socialist and Co-operative ideals; many desired to reform the marriage laws, not to abolish them; many remained extremely timid in their advocacy of the vote and, even if they had the courage to go as far as the suffrage, were careful to narrow their demand for it to widows and spinsters and to exclude married women. Few indeed were willing to advocate the election of women to Parliament. Some even refused to admit the possibility of their entering the higher professions. Nevertheless, the work of Thompson and Mrs Wheeler exercised a profound influence in crystallizing the latent stirrings for a fuller life, notably among the important section of women influenced by Socialist propaganda who took an active share in building up the Co-operative Movement, and especially its trading stores. The *Appeal* was a landmark in history.

10

Debating with John Stuart Mill

During the eighteen-twenties Thompson was often in London, where his tireless propaganda gave impetus to the rapidly expanding Co-operative Movement. He was the driving force in the historic debates of the Co-operators which began at Chancery Lane in 1825 and were later transferred to Red Lion Square. It is believed that the term 'Socialism' was first coined at these debates;[1] they were largely devoted to an examination of the various economic and social theses expounded in *An Inquiry into the Principles of the Distribution of Wealth* and included such topics as:

May not the greater part of the moral and physical evils which now afflict mankind be traced to individual competition in the production and distribution of wealth?

Is the labourer entitled to the whole product of his labour and why in the present state of society is the lot of the producing classes that of poverty and wretchedness?

What are the objections to a state of voluntary equality of wealth and community of property, and can they be satisfactorily answered?

What is the best mode of educating and training children?

Is it desirable in the formation of a social community to place the females in a state of perfect equality as to rights and powers?

Is the statement of Mr Malthus that 'Population has a tendency to increase faster than the Means of Subsistence' an insuperable barrier to the Co-operative System?

Is the position of Mr Owen correct that man is not properly the subject of praise, of blame, reward or punishment?

Can Eloquence and Poetry be usefully employed in the promulgation of Truth and in the diffusion of Happiness?

What are the ends which enlightened men would propose in the formation of a Social community?

The young John Stuart Mill, then in his late 'teens, had just founded the Utilitarian Society, when early in 1825 he learnt from John Roebuck of these Co-operative debates. He records in his *Autobiography* that he and most of his circle decided on going there in a body and 'having a general battle.' They found that the 'principal champion' on the Co-operative side was 'Mr Thompson of Cork.' Young Mill, evidently in no wise offended by the Irishman's forthright attack on the elder Mill's reactionary attitude to the women's question, subsequently referred to Thompson as 'a very estimable man with whom I was well acquainted.' Charles Austin opened the case for the Utilitarians, and the fight was kept up by adjournment before crowded audiences, including, along with members of the Co-operative Society and their friends, many hearers and some speakers from the Inns of Court. The speakers included William Ellis, Charles Villiers, Gale Jones, and Connup Thirlwell, whom Mill considered the best speaker he had ever heard. It was, he relates, 'a *lutte corps à corps* between Owenites and political economists,' whom the Co-operators regarded as 'their most inveterate opponents'; but it was 'a perfectly friendly dispute. We who represented political economy had the same objects in view as they had, and took pains to show it.'

The Chancery Lane debates left a lasting impression on many minds. A quarter of a century later the Christian Socialist, Frederick Denison Maurice, recalled them when talking with his disciple Minter Morgan, who noted that the pristine ideas first discussed in those days were 'in some degree answerable for the present doings of the Christian Socialists'; a dinner with Louis Blanc evoked similar thoughts in the mind of Roebuck, who considered that the Frenchman had merely revived the ideas of Thompson and his friends, and 'could not help exclaiming, "we have gone over the whole of this rubbish twenty years since."'

Another instrument of Thompsonite propaganda was the *Co-operative Magazine*, which was founded by the London Co-operative Society as the principal organ of their movement. Thompson seems to have been one of the founders of the journal and to have written the opening editorial. On another occasion he took the opportunity afforded by the publication by John Powell of a pamphlet on *The Causes of the Present Crisis* to draw attention to the fact that Powell had provided statistics to prove that real wages had fallen by half during the three decades between 1794 and 1824. Unlike Powell, who viewed the problem purely in financial terms, he argued that this rapid increase in misery was the result of the Industrial Revolution, the replacement of hand-made production by mechanized industries, the 'overwhelming pressure of taxation,' and the 'arbitrary' revaluation of the currency. Rebutting the claim of the orthodox economists, who, in vindicating the introduction of machinery, usually shut their eyes to the large-scale unemployment and falling wages which it often produced, he urged that the rosy picture conjured up by the economists was 'contradicted by the everyday experience of every person who will use his senses, and look out of books into the world.' Political economists forgot that each member of the working class could be starved only once in his life. There was 'an always-acting tendency' for change to succeed so rapidly to change that the forces of equilibrium were becoming more powerful than those which made for equilibrium.

Another issue of the *Magazine* carried an address to the 'Members of Mechanics' Institutes' in which Thompson declared that the time had come 'to consider seriously' how 'these stupendous machines' might be '*most usefully directed* so as to produce the greatest quantity of improvement and happiness.'[2] As in his pamphlet of a decade earlier, he criticized the Institutes which were then springing up on the ground that many of them were being perverted for the benefit of the managers and their friends. The mechanics, he declared, 'thirsted' for self-government, which would foster self-respect, free inquiry, and the desire for knowledge. They needed encouragement, not punishments, for any errors they committed would proceed from lack of experience, not from perverse or selfish reasons. With characteristic enthusiasm, he exhorted:

> Mechanics! govern yourselves; regulate your own affairs, employ *permanent* teachers; communicate knowledge impartially to all. Do this, and you will make your Institution really useful – one of the most powerful means of regenerating the human race.

Such ardent support for the education of the common people contrasts greatly with the contemporary attitude of many of his class. His was the age in which a clergyman asserted that workmen would not say their prayers if they became 'too scientific,' and when the Press wrote satires of society ladies forced to make the beds of servants out on sketching tours, while their husbands, members of the House of Lords, were obliged to carry their own parcels from the laundry because of coachmen away at lectures on astronomy. The Poet Laureate, Southey, expressed more than his own opinion when he wrote that he was 'no friend' of Mechanics' Institutes or of the University of London, as they would 'prepare the way for the overthrow of the Church.'[3]

Thompson, on the other hand, urged that concrete steps should be taken to strengthen secular education and minimize the influence of bourgeois forces. He argued that rich donors to Mechanics' Institutes should not be allowed to use their gifts as sordid bargaining counters; it should be obligatory for at least two-thirds of the managers to be composed of mechanics. These self-governing committees of management might well serve as umpires on industrial arbitration boards. This would be an improvement on Lord Cloncurry's proposal of an arbitration court with mercantile umpires. Both proposals were in advance of their time, for though embryo conciliation boards existed in France before this period, they did not make their appearance in Britain until 1850.

11

A Co-operative Approach to Politics

A few months after the Chancery Lane debates Thompson returned to Ireland to write a reply to Thomas Hodgskin's *Labour Defended*, which was then exerting considerable influence among London workmen. Thompson's reply, which was written under the *nom de plume* 'One of the Idle Classes,' took almost three years to complete, as 'almost a month was lost with every proof sheet' owing to the slow pace of communication between his home in Cork and the printers in London. It finally appeared in 1827 with the title *Labour Rewarded – the Claims of Labour and Capital Conciliated; or, How to Secure to Labour the Whole Products of its Exertions.*

The book, which was widely quoted in the early Co-operative and Socialist movement and later in Chartist circles, criticized the importance given by Hodgskin to '*mental* labourers, *literati*, men of science' and other 'non-productive labourers, whom the latter had classified as 'productive' on the ground that they earned their upkeep. This argument had been useful in rebutting the theory that the labourer must produce a profit for his employers in addition to his own subsistence, but opened the way to classifying capitalists and landlords as 'productive' on account of their entrepreneur function. Thompson's analysis of the economic system did not, however, differ radically from that of Hodgskin, who was in fact largely following the path he had himself laid down. Both writers attacked the exactions of landlords and capitalists, but while the Irish Socialist proposed the replacement of Capitalism by Co-operative Communism, Hodgskin sought to render the existing system completely competitive in the hope that this would enable the labourer to receive the full fruit of his toil. Thompson applauded this goal, but thought the means totally unrealistic. It was, he argued, 'entirely illusory' to assess the work accomplished by each labourer, however much such a calculation might be 'worshipped' by the 'supporters of the competitive system.' They and their 'chorus' were in fact 'fully assured' that 'no practical realization of this aim would reach the labourer.' Their recognition of the principle was 'as unreal as the shouts for liberty of the constitutional opportunists.'[1]

In his introduction Thompson explains that he had written his book 'to aid in bringing about a total change in the present principle of society regarding the production, accumulation, and distribution of wealth, and to substitute new principles of action more tending to universal comfort and happiness.' One of the first social critics to emphasize that the trade cycle was an inevitable malady of Capitalism, he asserted that as long as the existing system remained 'crisis will succeed to crisis at intervals more or less distant.' The time had come to abandon mere 'palliatives,' 'to cast aside the little expedients of the day and of the year, and to seek for a radical, a permanent cure of the evils that afflict society.' The 'permanent, everyday, chronic evils of the system,' which continued between its paroxysms, emphasized the need for 'a new principle of action' which would 'produce more abundantly all the good imputed to the present principle, and for ever avert its permanent as well as its passing evils.' Once the 'industrious classes' realized that the competitive system 'neither can nor professes to make more than a few happy, and that at the expense of the vast majority' it would become evident to them that 'it is imperative to their interest to seek out a system of industry, an honest object of which shall be to promote the happiness of all by giving to all abundantly and equally the means of acquiring happiness.'[2]

Labour Rewarded is less theoretical than the *Inquiry*, its arguments being couched in clear and forceful terms which every worker could understand. It declares that the capitalists who hypocritically proclaim the need for unequal remuneration on grounds of incentive, themselves were merely 'lucky or dexterous in the tricks and overreachings of exchanges.'[3]

The weight of Thompson's criticism fell on the political economists, who, he argued, had forgotten that mere 'increase of wealth,' if unaccompanied by happiness, ceased to be an 'object of rational desire.' Their whole attention had hitherto been almost exclusively directed to the creation of cheaper articles and to the creation of new masses of wealth in large and glittering heaps. Drawing a parallel between society and a beehive, he argued that the desire of the economists to allow 'free competition' among the 'Industrious Classes' was purely actuated by the hope that these classes might produce more honey, so that, after keeping themselves in a state fit for reproduction, a greater surplus might be left to be devoured by the drones or Idle Classes. The theories of the economists were a rationalization of the selfish interests of those who hoped to make their fortunes by 'raising themselves to affluence out of the degradation of the labouring classes and to succeed to the influence of the feudal and capitalist aristocracy by forming a new aristocracy, *the aristocracy of talent*.' Free competition was meaningless unless it were taken to imply that everyone at the outset of his career possessed equal wealth and knowledge, equal freedom of action and equal access to the means of production. 'Free competition between the son of a capitalist, inheriting of course the "merits" of his father, the merits of £20,000 a year, and the son of a labourer possessing nothing' was a sham. The advocates of competition admitted that under their supposedly ideal system 'the great mass of the human race must eternally remain greatly inferior in point of comforts to the few who will eternally rise by the chances of competition, or by what these partisans are pleased to call the *superior merits* of their exertions':

There is not a slave-driver who will not swear ' "tis idle to expect exertion from any other motives than the dread of the whip.' There are no competitive political economists who will not swear that it is idle to expect human exertion from any other motives than the pleasures of being above others and the striving to get up to others who are in point of wealth above themselves. The persuasion of the slave-driver and of the competitionist has been equally and necessarily formed by the circumstances surrounding each.

Economists were too naive when they wrote of the value of low wages. 'The real public, the vast majority of every community,' were and must be 'producers as well as consumers'; it could not therefore be to 'their interest that labour should be wretchedly remunerated.'[4]

Where one class of labourers was better paid than another it depended on the fluctuations of the market. Wages in a given industry might be higher or lower because of past circumstances, but the mere passage of time did not impart morality; it was fairer to conclude that reform was long overdue! To what particular class a child was born was outside its control. Moreover, skill depended on instruction and habit, not on higher wages, for unequal remuneration could not radically alter the different capacities of individuals. Higher pay for the skilled caused the higher income groups to despise the lower, thereby producing jealousy and unhappiness. To the contention that inequality was necessary to stimulate output, he protested like

Sismondi that over-exertion was the crying evil of factory life, destroying health, shortening life, and precluding the possibility of intellectual and educational improvement; it rendered life 'an eternal and feverish struggle: with the great majority, a hopeless struggle.'

It could not be said that the most hard-working and meritorious were the best paid, the opposite being in fact the case. Nor were extra wages awarded to the producers of essentials, for they were often more wretchedly paid than workers employed in the luxury trades. Nor did inequality of remuneration serve as compensation for unpleasant work, the most objectionable operations being always accompanied by starvation wages. In chimney-sweeping, for example, wretched children were '*compelled* to wear out their lives before manhood, or even youth,' while their wretched gains were pocketed by their 'scarcely less wretched masters.' 'Were justice the inspirer of unequal remuneration, its bounty would be dispensed to cheer the hardships of rugged and ungrateful toil.'

Unlike the Saint-Simonians, who ridiculed 'mathematical equality' and advocated a system in which the members of society would be arranged hierarchically in conformity with their social value and rewarded according to their work, Thompson remained a passionate apostle of equality. He argued that no ideal schedule of wages other than that of equality was possible. The factors on which such a schedule would have to depend were too complex for measurement and were subject to continuous change. The Industrial Revolution had already destroyed the high wages of many crafts which had previously taken a lifetime to acquire. No species of labour, if 'cheerfully given according to the capacity of the giver,' should be 'more, or less deserving of reward than any other.' Merit was its own reward; to reward it by extra remuneration was to interfere with 'security' and to take 'from the more needy to benefit the less needy.' Special keenness should not be rewarded; all labour ought to be a voluntary act, and would be so in a rational society from which idleness was banished, 'the pleasures of exertion or the favourable opinions of his companions' being reward enough for every man.[5]

The capitalist system, moreover, could 'never effect a just remuneration, even though equal laws and equal knowledge might prevail'; to attempt it would 'overturn the system of competition,' which by its very nature depended on the 'higgling of the market.'[6] It was therefore necessary to 'seek some other master principle to keep the great wheel of industry in motion, and to make it subservient to the happiness of all.'

Turn to what side we will, examine the matter as we may, under the system of Labour by individual competition, we must resort to the mere 'higgling of the market.' Chance and caprice will always be the sovereign regulators: but the springs of this higgling will be always kept in the hands of the adepts, and they will be so regulated, that prizes there will still be, and those prizes will fall into the hands of the most skilful in the higgling exchanges of competition; and there-fore, in nine cases out of ten, into the hands of the least benevolent. The present great object of human pursuit ought therefore to be to find out institutions and arrangements which would make the mag-nificent prodigality of means, of mechanical and other physical improvements which we possess, tributary to those great social improvements on which alone human happiness can securely repose.[7]

The basic feature of the age, Thompson explained, was that the domestic economy was being replaced by competitive Capitalism. In the past the lot of the workers had been 'seclusion, ignorance and toil,' but though they had 'produced but little, by far the greater part of that little was consumed by themselves.' Since then the industrial and commercial revolutions had almost 'entirely undersold and broken up the ancient arrangements,' though they had survived in tailoring, shoemaking, hatting, carpentry, and printing, where labour was still not performed on a large scale by machinery, and where wages were the highest and most steady. Some 'friends of the industrious classes,' looking only at 'the fair side' of the old order and comparing it with 'the vicissitudes, the miseries and the vices' attendant on the new, wished to give up the benefits of cheap production and 'to chain down or regulate the gigantic efforts of mechanical skill and individual exer-tion'; this attempt to bring back a system which had 'gone, never to return,' stemmed from 'sickly and ignorant good nature'; 'enlightened wisdom' would 'give up no real benefit that the progress of civilization' had produced, but would 'look out for the means of retaining the whole of the benefit, avoiding its casually attendant evils.' Only Co-operation could thus synthesize the advantages of the domestic system with those of machinery; it was the only system which would allow manufactures to 'be again domesticated' and reconciled with increasing knowledge and universal intercourse. The golden age of the future would 'include a thousand times more than all the advantages' hitherto afforded by the 'supposed happy and simple' domestic system;

there would be the utmost possible mechanization, enabling costs to fall and human drudgery to be minimized, while all the evils hitherto inherent in industrialization would be banished, and all its benefits 'shared equally and immediately by all.'

Labour Rewarded contains a lengthy review of the proposals of reform canvassed in early nineteenth-century England; though its author is sympathetic to many of them, he regards them as 'palliatives,' observing that they all fail to attack the competitive system, which retards, and renders impossible 'any high state of social and individual happiness.'

The introduction of democracy was the most necessary reform after the establishment of Co-operation, for it would 'bring with it all other reforms.' Co-operation was 'entirely friendly' to this 'grand experiment,' and, though Co-operators need not have any political or religious creed, they could not reason logically if they opposed it. There was, moreover, some sense in demanding political reform as a step to Co-operation, because it would be exceedingly valuable if legislation could be the prerogative of the workers. True representatives of the people, removable by the popular will, would abolish legislation hostile to Co-operation and make loans to assist Co-operative projects. After the advent of Co-operation, democracy would still be essential as a safeguard against corruption and arbitrary practices. Only the 'Industrious Classes' should make the laws affecting their happiness, as no one else possessed 'a sufficiently broad basis of sympathy to make beneficent laws.'

The establishment of democracy would not, however, destroy 'the root of inequality and wretchedness.' It would be unwise to suppose:

as did the simple French at the time of their (as yet) abortive revolution, as do the equally simple American people, that the mere naming, by the industrious classes, of men to make public regulations to promote their happiness, would necessarily secure that object, or would even in any material degree secure to them the use of the products of their labour.[8]

Thompson's appreciation of the value of the parliamentary franchise for the working classes, despite his realization that Socialism would not automatically arrive with the winning of the vote, contrasted strongly with the attitude of Owen who declared that it was of 'no consequence whether governments were despotic or not.'

Labour Rewarded provides a sketch of an ideal system of government which aimed at obtaining the maximum of freedom with the minimum of coercion and bureaucracy. It draws attention to the evils of over-centralization in which 'the fortunes and happiness of millions of men in all parts of an extensive country' are subordinated to 'the caprices of a few hundred persons, living or occasionally meeting in a capital city, making war, levying taxes, issuing edicts or laws without knowledge of or sympathy with the wants or wishes of the people who are lightly called "Provincials," or "the country."' To obviate these evils the people should form themselves into communes and elect Provincial, State, and National Legislatures. Every law would have to be passed by majority vote in the Assembly of the administrative unit concerned, and also receive the assent of a majority of the smaller units which comprised that unit. Any unit conceiving its interests endangered by the laws of another unit would appeal to the unit above them, and any legislature which found its wishes frustrated by less than a two-thirds majority in the higher body would have the right to call for a referendum of all the communes. The executive and judiciary would be elected by popular suffrage and be subject to recall;[9] no government officials would have the power to veto any law, involve the inhabitants in war, or do 'any other mischief' without the consent of a majority of communes and a majority of Provincial Legislatures as well as the consent of the National Assembly. Civil and criminal law would be codified and published; case law, based on the vagaries and inconsistencies of judicial decisions, would be abolished. No authority would have the power of enforcing its regulations by any punishments other than 'the ultimate penalty' of exile.

Under such a system no power being reserved to enforce the execution of unjust or unequal laws, reason and the interest of those whom laws affect must be the sole guides. No local barbarisms could exist; no jealousies between the national or state legislatures, nor between the different states, provinces or communes; knowledge would be universally diffused; individual happiness would at length become the avowed and real object of legislation.[10]

Thompson's views on the law may have owed something to the systematic analysis of Bentham, who had declared that jurisprudence was a 'system of abomination' which required a Luther to subject it to that 'full and general abhorrence which must take place before any effectual reform can be accomplished.' 'One of the Idle Classes' indicted the complications, delays, and cost of the law as 'devised by one set of the Idle Classes, or what is worse, the perniciously busy class, the lawyers, to enable them to share with another set, the capitalists, as large a portion as possible of their annual abstractions from the products of labour.' The 'abuses of the law' gave an 'enormous means of oppression to the Idle Classes in their disputes with the Industrious' and made it possible for them to keep down wages. Political power was 'vested in the same individuals (or their dependants), in glaring and audacious ridicule of the idle declamations of the very same individuals respecting the benefits of a strict separation of powers.'

> The game laws alone, in which the same individuals are lawmakers, judges, executioners and parties, are enough to unhumanize any country, not to speak of the tithe laws, the corn laws, and the thousand other Acts by which magistrates trample down the happiness of the Industrious Classes at their pleasure.

Laws should be 'mild, simple, as few as possible and intelligible to all whose interests they affect.' Parties to a dispute should be personally interrogated by the judges, who should be popularly elected; professional lawyers and 'the whole tribe of our law agents' should cease to exist. Tithe laws, corn laws, and the rest of 'the thousand other Acts' which trampled down the workers should be repealed, and 'nothing substituted in their place.' Such reforms, however, would remove only 'those obstacles out of the way of the Industrious Classes which prevent them from attaining that portion of the products of their labour which free competition might afford them.' The skill of all employed workers would 'still compete' against itself; the 'eternal underbidding of the worst remunerated' and the 'ever advancing improvements in machinery and chemical combinations' would continue to 'throw new bodies of the industrious out of employment.'[11]

Educational reform deserved enthusiastic support, the more so as 'every consistent advocate of Co-operation' must realize that the diffusion of knowledge would assist in winning the support of the working class, who as they became enlightened came more and more to understand the importance of Co-operation. Mechanics' Institutes should at once be extended to all small towns and to the country, so as to be available to agriculturalists as well as to artisans, to rural labourers as well as townspeople. Discussion of social science should be encouraged instead of forbidden or frowned upon. It was necessary, however, to take a saner view than the 'Society for the Diffusion of Useful Knowledge,' which assumed that its own favourite panacea was the sole necessity for social happiness, and whose supporters often declaimed against active measures for political and social improvement as altogether unnecessary.[12]

Free trade in corn would not radically ameliorate the condition of the workers. 'Three-fourths, not to say nine-tenths of the benefits' would be 'reaped by the exchangers, wholesale and retail, the master-carriers, and the master-manufacturers'; the competitive system, which allowed the workers only to reap 'the gleanings of their exertions,' would always lower the wages of labour in accordance with the cost of living. There was no evidence that the cheapening of manufactured articles by machinery had raised the remuneration of the labourer, nor was there any 'necessary connection' between 'cheapness of food and ample remuneration of labour.' The Irish peasants, and the Russian serfs who were 'fed by the benignity of the lord and sold with the land,' were utterly wretched, though the price of food was extremely low in their countries. A parallel to the proposed abolition of the Corn Laws had been afforded by the abolition of tithes in Scotland, in which country the landlords alone had derived any advantage; 'whether, as in England and Ireland, the tithes have been retained, or, as in Scotland and most parts of the continent of Europe, they have been abolished, by one expedient or another the Idle Classes seize on nine-tenths if not ninety-nine hundredths of the benefit.'[13]

It was most unlikely that 'prudential population checks, moral or physical,' could alone accomplish 'even the pitiful object of their partisans.' Any advantage secured by restricting the numbers in a given occupation or area would swiftly be overwhelmed by an influx of competitors from elsewhere; moreover, the capitalist could always move his capital in search of cheaper labour. Employers might also take advantage of the limited size of the worker's family to reduce his wages; were wages geared to the needs of someone who restricted his family, they might fall beneath the subsistence level of those with large families to support. Furthermore, since no labourer could predict employment prospects a generation ahead, he could not arrange the number of his children accordingly; in drawing attention to this last point Thompson was again adopting an argument put forward by Sismondi a few years earlier.

The Irish Socialist went on to oppose the then much-advocated project of a cottage tax to deter population growth. It would be an additional factor in forcing people to abandon the countryside for the towns. Even were a corresponding tax placed on urban dwellings any slight advantage would be offset by the miseries of overcrowding which would be accentuated. He also rejected the suggestion of a marriage tax, which had obtained the support both of Sismondi and Thomas Rowe Edmonds, protesting that it would have to be graduated to income if it were not unduly to penalize the poor; even then it would be a 'tyranny truly worthy of competitive genius.' Carried out by 'our amiable fox-hunting and tithe-collecting magistrates,' it would be 'the first step, and no small one, towards a pure white slave system, tried and guaranteed for the British oligarchy by foreign despots whose people are reduced in intellect almost to the level of our genuine black slaves.' Even were cottages taxed, breeding could be carried out in garrets; were marriage licenses refused, it could proceed without them.[14]

The difficulties should not, however, mean that individual prudence should be cast aside either in contracting marriage or in the multiplication of children. Marriage laws should be remodelled to render them perfectly equal between the sexes, and the relationship should be terminable at the wish of either party. People who had produced one child outside legal wedlock should no longer be obliged to marry, thereby adding half a dozen additional paupers to the one already produced. Primogeniture should be abolished, so that parents desirous of maintaining estates intact would be forced to practise family limitation.

Proposals for emigration did not 'pretend to cure the evils of our internal organization,' but left them 'just where they found them.' To achieve an appreciable rise in wages, some 300,000 persons would have to leave the United Kingdom every year, a number which was 'utterly impracticable' for financial and shipping reasons. Such an exodus would operate on wages like the 'non-breeding plan.' Capitalists interested in 'keeping wages down to the mere existence level' would 'never permit emigration to raise wages so high as to endanger their competition with the low wages paid by foreign capitalists. Long before any substantial good was done to the industrious classes, the moment mere starvation was averted, the influence of capitalists would arrest emigration.' Colonization schemes were from every point of view a cheat. 'The only rational' plan would be to enable 'the emigrants *to supply each other's needs* not only for food, but of clothing, shelter and furniture.' This could be done by exporting a suitable 'assortment of tradespeople and manufacturers with tools, machinery and materials or the means of procuring them,' but this was 'not contemplated by our competitive friends of emigration,' who either thought that it was too costly or that it would destroy their hope of exporting to the emigrants, should they survive, the very articles which the emigrants themselves, properly organized and supplied, would make abroad for a half or a third of the cost of imported goods.[15]

Labour Rewarded gives qualified support to proposals of tax reduction, the stabilization of the currency, and various forms of insurance. It emphasizes, however, that these are merely 'palliatives.' Tax reform would benefit the rich more than the extremely poor who paid no taxes; moreover, the average *per capita* tax payment was only £4 or £5 a year, compared with £100 which the productive classes paid to the unproductive in the form of rent and profits. 'Arbitrary alterations in the currency' were a powerful factor making for 'the misery of the labouring classes,' but the advocates of monetary reform were 'eternally deluding' the people when they claimed that it would substantially improve their position. Voluntary insurance schemes were of little use to the poorest and most needy sections of the population, offered no relief for permanent incapacity, did not envisage raising the status and wages of women, and could not even maintain the contributor during a period of prolonged unemployment or support his children if orphaned. It was 'strange' that the advocates of such petty schemes were often 'enemies of mutual co-operation,' which was 'nothing less than a complete system of universal insurance against all casualties.'[16]

12

Trade Unionism

Before the repeal of the Combination Acts, Thompson argued that it was 'horribly cruel and contradictory' for the defenders of existing society to declare that there was 'in the nature of things an impassable limit' to wages and at the same time to keep them down by legislative action.[1] The fact that English workers would 'rather risk life itself than submit to the incredible privations of the Irish peasant' and that so many American labourers had saved enough to become small capitalists, thereby creating the 'cheering spectacle of a scarcity of servants,' proved 'the utter falsehood' of the view of the economists that wages could not rise above subsistence level.[2]

In *Labour Rewarded*, which was written immediately after the legalization of trade unions, Thompson revealed himself a strong supporter of the movement, which he referred to as 'the most interesting' and 'by far the most important' of his time. His interest preceded that of Robert Owen, who ignored its significance until he formed his shortlived 'Grand National Consolidated Trade Union' some seven or so years later. The approach of Thompson, and later of Owen, contrasted greatly with that of the propagandists of privilege and reaction, who continued to condemn workmen's combinations as 'pernicious.' 'One of the Idle Classes' bitterly reproached those who had no other remedy for the evils of the competitive system except 'the thinning of the number of the industrious'; he utterly refused to agree with Nassau Senior's harsh recommendation that 'peaceful picketing' should 'be comprehensively forbidden and ruthlessly punished' and that 'employers or their assistants' should have the right 'to arrest men without summons or warrant and to hale them before any Justice of the Peace.'[3]

To Thompson the flaw in the unions was not the pressure they might bring to bear on the employer but their inability to procure adequate remuneration for their members. He contended that under 'Free Competition' they could never secure the workers 'anything like the products of their labour,' but only such remuneration as would permit the capitalists in one line of industry to reap the average rate of profits. If the union demanded more than this an employer would transfer his capital elsewhere. Not even 'the really benevolent capitalist' would pay more, since he would be undersold by his rivals at home or abroad. Unionist strength was, moreover, limited to times of prosperity, for during trade depressions, the mass of misery was so immense that provision of adequate relief was altogether impossible, and the worker's solidarity with his fellows was liable to break down.[4]

Nevertheless, unionism had a vital role to play. It could prevent 'individual competition among the workmen,' and thereby stop wages in any particular firm being forced below the remuneration elsewhere. Anyone victimized by a particular employer could be supported while out of work; 'a very strong bar' would thus be provided against unjustifiable wage reductions and acts of oppression on the part of individual employers. Every member of the 'Industrious Classes' ought to become a member.

While championing those trade unions which were open to all and merely united the workers against their employers, Thompson assailed those whose exclusive membership prevented the unskilled from entering a better-paid trade. To limit the number of apprentices or to aim at excluding 'poor foreigners' was both vain and unjust. It was a conspiracy which would divide the well-paid from the ill-paid and, if carried to its logical conclusion, would lead to bloodshed, in which the unskilled would 'everywhere form a league with the capitalists' and use their numerical superiority and the support of the State to defeat the interests of exclusiveness.[5]

To overcome these animosities and to strengthen the workers' position as against capital there should be formed a 'central union of all the general unions of all the trades of the country.' Its central fund should be used to assist the unemployed in any area or branch when funds were exhausted, and a wage schedule should be drawn up to compensate for local variations in prices and conditions of work which would otherwise render national wages unjust. 'The Central Union' would have to 'extend its operations and enlarge its sympathies' so as to cater for the entire British working class – including the agricultural labourers, who might at first be hard to organize in the face of 'the frowns of the landlords.' Later the herculean labour of forming international trade unionism would have to be considered. Trade unionism, Thompson concluded, was destined to be a vital factor in the emancipation of the working class and in teaching them the need for Communism. It would call the intellectual powers of its members 'into full activity on subjects most directly concerning their happiness, but hitherto neglected.' Each labourer, instead of looking upon his fellows as his competitors, his rivals, and enemies, would come to sympathize with their wants and would regard himself as linked to them by similarity of employment, pursuits, and interest. Universal goodwill could not 'prevail between the Idle and the Industrious Classes'; but their mutual jealousies and antipathies could be softened, and an opening afforded for reason to convince both sides of their real interests in Universal Union.[6] Trade unions could help the industrious classes by promoting the acquisition of capital which could be used in Co-operative production. Buildings and machinery should be erected to give work to the unemployed, instead of merely supporting them in 'demoralizing idleness.' This would 'be something approaching an efficient check on the exactions of capitalists, and would prove that capital could be accumulated without them. To remove the last exactions of landlords and merchants and to abolish the uncertainties of competition and bad trade, Co-operation itself would have to be introduced. Trade unions would thus evolve into communities of Co-operation.

13

Attitude to Religion

Thompson and the early Socialists found the clergy their irreconcilable foes on all the issues they held dear. Clerical opposition extended from purely theological questions to most fields of social and economic life. It was not uncommon for parsons to refuse the use of church halls to Co-operative organizers, to preach sermons against Socialism, and to raise the cry of 'atheist materialism'; a Co-operative tract of 1832 writes of the 'obloquy and calumny' which Owen and Thompson suffered for their religious views; burial services were on occasion denied to their followers; and William Pare, one of the Irishman's chief disciples, was deprived of his post as Registrar of Births, Deaths, and Marriages in Birmingham on the intervention of the Bishop of Exeter.[1] The Co-operators were not slow to retaliate. They assailed the dogmas of Christianity in innumerable tracts, and in a single year held no less than fifty formal debates with the clergy.

Thompson was from the first an avowed Rationalist and an anticlerical fully confident that reason must ultimately triumph over the dogmas of alleged revelation. He declared that truth could not be unaccompanied by evidence. Religions were 'false by their own showing' in that 'they acknowledged themselves incompetent to operate on conviction' alone, and relied also on violence, persecution, child-indoctrination, and other extraneous means of persuasion. They admitted that unless thus supported 'even the unbiased reason of children would never receive them, though God himself were their author and advocate.' For the most part, they were a 'heterogeneous medley of wisdom and folly, truth and fable'; 'an enormous mass of puerile dogmas, visions and dreams,' mixed up with 'regulations made by able barbarians for a barbarous state of society.' It was 'fortunate for knowledge and for mankind' that 'so little' had been 'known or even dreamed of at the time the holy books were penned,' for that was the only factor limiting the extent to which knowledge was made to wither at the touch of superstition. Which religion a man subscribed to depended not on the will of God, but on the environment in which he was brought up. If a Turkish and an Irish child were exchanged in infancy the Irish Mohammedan would grow up to look with horror at Christians as 'monsters who worshipped three gods' and whose priests 'ordained or compounded the divine nature' in the Communion service.[2]

Priests were 'rapacious parasites'; 'ghostly dealers in creeds and spiritual brimstone,' they insolently and hypocritically 'monopolized the moral teaching of society.' European theologians 'assured the blacks in their colonies and the slaves of fraud, force or competition whom they kept down at home, "*that the Lord had called them to their respective stations in life*," and that it was "the duty of *unwilling* slaves to be meekly obedient and satisfied with their wretchedness"'; the same clergy turned upon 'the *willing* victims of superstition in Hindustan' and assured them that the Lord had 'not called them to their state of life' and that he utterly disapproved of their submission. The European priests happened 'to have no interest in wife burning,' the benefits of which were monopolized by their Brahmin 'cousin theologians,' otherwise there would have been 'an ordinance of the Lord' to enforce it. He would have been 'as friendly to it as to submission to any other species of oppression.'[3]

The clergy cheated the people with pretences, with 'the rotten pretended nails of the true cross' and other commercially exploited fakes. Belief in the dogmas of the priests was of paramount importance not to their 'dupes' but to themselves, for unless the 'dupes' deemed the dogmas 'of more importance than the world's wealth,' how could the priests 'succeed in monopolizing such immense portions of it for themselves?' On the supposition that a supernatural being existed, it could not 'in any way affect the happiness of the author of Nature or be anything but a matter of indifference to him how his creatures speculated as to his essence or attributes.' The Quakers were the only sect 'wise enough' to be their own priests, and thus save the expense of a separate order who had no real duties but invented imaginary ones to delude the people into making 'forced contributions.' Tithes were 'the most pernicious of taxes' – they did not produce 'any public benefit,' but merely enabled the priests or clergy to 'gorge themselves.'[4]

Religions were pernicious, both because they were used by the excessively rich to perpetuate their power and wealth, and because they were irrational and hence an incubus on the free development of the human mind. Speculations were 'idle' when there was 'no data for judging.' To attempt, as did the Saint-Simonians, to place religion in the service of education or human happiness was 'worse than useless,' for it distracted people's attention from the real reasons why progress was desirable; such a policy was bound to fail, as was proved both by 'experience and reason.'

All laws should pass the test of utility, not of religion:

> No code or law ought to be permitted to continue its mischiefs because a man in a time of ignorance, Mahomet or any other, said he went into a swoon or dream of what he calls the seventh heaven. If Mahomet, or still more if God, whose sentiments Mahomet says he speaks, has any good reasons in favour of the code or laws surely such reasons could be given; otherwise omniscience is converted into stupidity.[5]

Thompson was confident that the future progress of society would witness the liberation of the human mind from the fetters of all superstition. The 'genuine morality' of utility, together with 'historical truth,' would ultimately supersede 'the pretended morality of self-debasement and mortification'; idle ceremonies and unintelligible, unimportant dogmas would be abandoned. With the advent of Communism 'the trade of religion, like the trade of law,' would gradually cease. Those who liked 'the heavenly wares' and 'the ghostly consolations' which priests retailed could in return make 'a voluntary exchange' of the produce of their labour; but the majority would soon realize that 'wholesome and palatable food, neat clothing and commodious houses, were more substantial blessings than promises of futurity and lands above the clouds'; they would keep the produce of their labour for themselves, and 'let the priests or apostles make tents or baskets, or follow any other calling for their honest support.' Competition would amend the morals of the clergy. As soon as religion became a purely personal and voluntary matter 'theologians would have no nation's plunder to fight for and no brutal force to give weight to their arguments or to exact their plunder.' Their disputes would 'become as harmless, if not as innocently interesting, as the famed Arabian stories of the thousand and one nights.'[6]

14

The Theory of Communities

The Co-operators of Thompson's day believed the good society could be brought about by a group of enthusiasts who would contract out of existing society, with all its degradations and immoralities, and demonstrate the benefits of a rationally constructed social organization. In their plans it is possible to read the story of a sometimes conscious, sometimes subconscious, revolt from the immoralities, inhumanities, and drudgeries of the new industrial civilization, with its wretchedly insanitary dwellings and workshops, the evils of child labour, the callous neglect of the health of workers, the uncertainties of trade depression, and the cruelly prolonged hours of labour. They rejected the fantastically unequal distribution of wealth of the era of early industrialism, protested against the exploitation of the labourer, and repudiated the materialism which conceived the worker not as a human personality but as a mere instrument of production, indistinguishable, as Thompson complains, from the ox or the spinning-jenny. They sought to subordinate the blind working of the economic system to humane and democratic values and to eradicate the pride of the rich and dictatorship of aristocratic government. They believed that human life was being poisoned because everyone sought private advantage to the detriment of all; that the play of economic forces must be rationalized, organized, and moralized; that society should have a conscious meaning; that town planning should be governed by the will of man, not merely by the working of impersonal economic forces or by the caprice of a handful of capitalists and factory owners; that economic uncertainty due to incapacity or death of the breadwinner could be brought to an end; that the illiteracy of the people must be terminated; that mechanization should not create surplus production and poverty in the midst of plenty, but eliminate poverty and render the hours of toil shorter and less burdensome. Above all, there was the idea that society must be recast; that individualistic life in isolated families would be replaced by the fuller life of Communism; that communal canteens, crèches, and infant schools would beneficially replace the system in which half the race is banished to the home, there to live a life economically unnecessary and intellectually idiotic; that such institutions as marriage, the family, and private property, which had grown up as a result of past environmental conditions, could now be transformed by rebuilding a new environment framed, not by the fortuities of history, but by rational decisions.

In Thompson's day there was not yet any discussion as to whether Socialism could be achieved in one country alone while surrounded by the capitalist world. The question then was whether the new system could be established in one district alone or required to be established over a whole country. Owen and Thompson thought they could set it up in one locality at a time, while the Saint-Simonians sought to bring it about in an entire country by means of Government action.

In England the idea of Socialist communities was a mushroom growth. It had not attracted much attention until the end of the Napoleonic wars, when Thompson was already forty years of age; yet by the time of his death, some eighteen years later, it had become the Messianic gospel of a Co-operative Movement with over 300 branches, and exerted a profound influence on many social reformers outside the confines of strictly Socialist thought. Though Owen was the originator of the idea of communities and had advocated them from 1816 onwards, Holyoake is right in referring to Thompson as 'the first systematic writer' on the subject.

In his *Inquiry into the Principles of the Distribution of Wealth* he argued that the establishment of communities would terminate the division of society into owners of capital and suppliers of labour. Everyone would be simultaneously a supplier of labour and an owner of capital, and 'in all transactions the greater interests, that of the labourer, would preponderate.' Production surpluses would no longer be a restraint on consumption, but would be disposed of in the interest of all. Such advantages as competition possessed might be maintained within the realm of inter-community trading, where they would keep prices down; but excessive underselling and price cutting would cease, for no community would export surplus produce for articles 'produced by less labour.'[1]

Exchanges would be based on estimates of the amount of labour employed in production. If no exact estimate were available 'mutual good faith' would 'arrange to the satisfaction of both parties.' Should the labour of either of the parties have been misapplied, and consequently be less productive than the average, it must suffer for the consequences: 'Otherwise a premium would be given to indolence, and the most idle and least skilful would be enabled to live at the expense of the industrious: to rate them at their proper standard would quicken the industry of all.'[2]

Unlike Owen, Thompson believed that the privileged holders of political power could not be expected to be more than 'indifferent' to Co-operation; they would oppose any betterment of the majority if it conflicted with their own 'supposed interests.' They regarded Co-operation as 'outside the pale of the law' and obliged Co-operators to protect their property by the 'miserable device' of registering it under the names of secretaries or other officials uncontrollable at law should they embezzle it.[3] Co-operators wished to establish their system by reason and argument, but the privileged classes would have to 'cease to be what they are before they would yield to such persuasion'; it was therefore 'the extreme of weakness to expect from them any more than reluctant submission.' Nevertheless, in practice their enmity could be discounted for 'political power, being already in conflict with the popular will, would find itself forced to embrace principles governed by free discussion, or would be subjected to the daily risk of attacks of force from secret combinations.' The old ways of government could no longer continue, because the truth had 'got abroad among the inhabitants of Europe that all political institutions ought to be tributary to the happiness of the majority, or at least of those whose interest they affect.' Neither compulsion nor delusion could therefore much longer govern the affairs of men. Communities would speedily become 'the general practice of society,' no one would dare to stand in their way.[4]

Turning to the future role of the State, the *Inquiry* argues more or less along Godwinian lines and anticipates the Marxian thesis of the withering away of the State. It claims that communities would 'supersede almost all the present institutions relating to law' because they would remove the causes of crime and force would no longer be needed to 'overawe' popular discontent. The immense sums expended on the law would be dispensed with; laws would 'execute themselves,' as all would co-operate to safeguard the common interest. Wars would cease, as there would be no more vested interests to profit from them. Taxation would be minimal, as those who levied contributions would themselves be the contributors; such taxes as would still be required would take the form of a rent, graduated to the wealth of each community. As 'the passion for individual accumulation and display of wealth' died down, 'almost all the ordinary functions of government would also have ceased.' The State would be 'superseded by the voluntary discharge of such of those duties as were found necessary within each separate community for its own benefit.'[5]

Thompson laid great emphasis on the role of public opinion, which in his communitarian plans was to replace the coercive nature of the State. He declared that public opinion had hitherto been nothing but 'the opinion of the influential classes of society, those whose opinions and conduct have most control and who influence the actions, and hence the happiness of their fellow creatures, by direct benefits or evils or by hope or terror.'[6] Despite the 'heroic exertions' of the few who had 'the sublime courage' to speak what they conceived to be the truth, enlightened public opinion had generally been overwhelmed by 'the defects of education and the perversity of institutions.' 'Vague declamations in the mouths of priests or philosophers about truth, justice and beneficence' had not 'weighed a feather' in the forming of character, because they had been opposed by practical examples of 'falsehood, rapine and cruelty' and had degenerated into 'inculcating habits of oppression.' Public opinion in communities would be radically different; never before had 'the wise and the good ever enjoyed such ample opportunity for directing a right public opinion.' The educational system would enable each member to 'comprehend and if necessary to direct' the whole establishment. All members would become 'as nearly as possible equally intelligent and equally capable of contributing to the common good.' Words and precepts would be of little use as 'motives to action' until a change had been brought about in the environment and institutions that gave rise to them.[7]

Thompson further elaborated the communitarian idea in the pages of *The Co-operative Magazine*. In 1826 he discussed a letter he had received from a correspondent who had argued that:

I do not go to the length of maintaining that Co-operation is *nationally* practicable; but I go this length, that the present stage of society will merge into purely military government *in its next change*; and that a perfect line of demarcation will be drawn between the *rich*, supported by their armies, and the *people*, united by their sense of degradation, their privations, and their sufferings. Rely upon it, nothing but the Co-operative system will prevent the terrible collision which is inevitable between the two classes; and no matter what are our individual predilections and opinions, no man will have a choice; he must join that side to which chance, or as Mr Owen says 'circumstance,' has attached him.

I do not think it possible to convert the dense mass of the population of cities and great towns into Co-operative villages, but I think that if the mass of the people in the country were so converted, a new and improved state of society would result.[8]

In his reply Thompson argued that communities should be formed 'not by agriculturalists alone to produce food, but by labourers and tradesmen of every description to supply each other with all the comforts as well as the necessities of life.' Towns would 'gradually become deserted' because people would leave them for communities and because co-operatively produced goods would drive all other goods off the market. The Co-operative system would thus obviate 'the enormous evils inseparable from the dense population of large towns,' as well as 'the evils of mother Nature attendant on isolated country dwellings.'

From this argument it was only a short step to town and country planning. He argued that 'the question as to whether mankind would be happier living in larger or smaller towns, or in the country, or in situations combining all the advantages and avoiding all the evils of both town and country' had never been given sufficient attention. The site of the dwellings of the many had been determined by 'the pecuniary interest or caprice of the few,' the many having 'no more choice in the place of their abode than bullocks in the pastures where they are fattened.' 'The freedom of choice for the poor under competition' was like 'the freedom of our Courts of Law open to all who can pay the price of admission, a price altogether out of the reach of those destitute of capital.' It was time that human affairs should be 'regulated by human reason, and taken out of the guidance of mere chance or caprice.' It was therefore a mistake for Owen to refer to Co-operative 'villages' and 'villagers'; such words had always been associated with ideas of poverty, lack of knowledge, uncouthness of manners, and dependence; they were inappropriate for communities which would be as unlike villages and their inhabitants as they would be 'unlike cities and those who now inhabit them.'[9]

Late in 1826 as part of his propaganda to win the workers to these ideas Thompson issued an *Address to the Industrious Classes of Great Britain*, which embodied its author's ideas on community building in concise terms and demonstrated the intimate relationship that existed between his critique of competitive society and his proposals for social reconstruction, vividly revealing the extent to which he was concerned with the need for society to develop a protective covering to shield itself from the economic blizzards of the competitive system. It declares that the old system is coming to a close as a result of the Industrial Revolution. The workers' struggle against the employers, who owned the means of production and controlled the legislature and the Press, was proving of no avail. Whenever an increase in wages was achieved, cheap labour was brought in from elsewhere. The solutions expounded by the politicians only scratched at the problem. What was needed was to terminate the system of exploitation, and this could only be achieved by means of Co-operation, which would enable the workers to become their own employers. A start could be made at once if those sympathetic would save from sixpence to five shillings weekly until an average of five pounds was accumulated for every adult and fifty shillings for every child under ten. The rest of the money required, a few thousand pounds, might be lent or given by persons who lived on the labour of others but who wished to inaugurate an era of 'equal and universal justice and happiness.' Savings would be deposited in a bank, and contributors should register as community members.

Thompson announced that it was intended to purchase some hundred acres that very winter; work would begin in the spring of 1827 'with any number of the industrious classes,' from 200 to 2,000. The time had arrived for the labourers to abandon short-sighted interests and to take into their own hands the running of their affairs:

> Resolve; make a beginning. Your own happiness and that of your descendants will be secured; the selfish principle of competition will soon everywhere give way to the benign principle of universal Co-operation. In this great work you will have the happiness of leading the way in England.

A few weeks later the *Co-operative Magazine* published a 'Prospectus of the Cork Co-operative Community,' which was to be erected 'within 15 miles' of Cork City. The 'Prospectus' drew attention to the fact that 'more than nine-tenths' of the products of labour were not consumed by the producers, but by 'paupers, wholesalers and retailers of all descriptions, carriers, employers, possessors of capital, owners of land, consumers of taxes, not to speak of law-supported trade monopolists, nor of the professors of healing, killing, or chicanery under the name of Law.'[10] Even the tenth which was available for the 'real producers' was always liable to be taken out of their hands by 'wars, bad seasons, imprudent speculations of merchants or manufacturers, the awakened industry of foreign nations, improvements in machinery at home or abroad, or domestic or foreign financial regulations.'

The Cork Co-operative Community would unite people in large numbers in one harmonious family without inequalities and clashes of interest which elsewhere tormented 'the very retreats of domestic life.' Members would not 'be pained by the sight or burdened by the support of paupers,' as everyone would be engaged in work 'appropriate to their particular talents and constitutions'; those incapacitated by disease, accident, or old age would as a matter of course be supported by their comrades. Members would be 'enabled to dispense with the services of wholesale and retail dealers' because they would themselves perform 'all that is useful in such offices'; they would 'dispense with carriers' because they would produce most bulky articles on their own land. They would 'do without employers' because they would be their own employers. They would be freed from the power of speculators because, 'not wishing to live on the labour of their fellow creatures,' they would refrain from speculation. They would possess a guaranteed market because they would 'afford a market to each other, producing and consuming the products of each other's labour.' They would 'do without the aid of lawyers' because 'the dissensions and contests arising from individual possession' would 'cease with the removal of their cause,' all minor disagreements being 'amicably arranged *within* the community.' They would avoid the expenses of doctors because 'the art of promoting health' would be developed. 'Undeviating temperance, perfect cleanliness of house and person, freedom from unhealthy employments and abundance of all useful things' would ensure health which was 'the indispensable basis of all other enjoyments.'

The community, which would 'ultimately' accord with the 'Articles of Agreement' drawn up by the London Co-operative Society in the previous year, would consist of some 2,000 members. Land would be taken at the rate of one acre for every individual. If a start were made with 200 adult members, fifty-two workers would be required for gardening and agriculture, sixty-six for building and furnishing, fifty-nine for textile manufactures, and twenty-three for miscellaneous work, baking, shoemaking, milling, storekeeping, and teaching. Full freedom could not appear at once; it would have to be deferred until the community was safely established. In the initial period members must work 'diligently' at whatever tasks might be allotted to them by the managers, though after the first year the community should be fully controlled by elected committees. Each committee would superintend its particular department, but would report to the general body of members. One member of each committee would retire every three months, and would not be re-eligible for a similar period. When not employed in committee work, everyone would have to engage in his or her ordinary manual work.

Community members would have to prepare themselves for austerity in the initial period. 'The milk of the cows on the land and the bread and potatoes made and prepared by the members and purchased out of their funds' would be the only food available for the first 200 days. Capital expenditure would have to be restricted to procure stock, machinery, and raw materials. Necessities would have to be produced before luxuries; no new clothes could be distributed until six months after work began. Even after the first year members must not consume 'more than three-fourths of their annual produce,' as the remainder would be needed to meet the rent, repay borrowed capital, and purchase more machinery.

Should the community find in its ranks 'any confirmed idler, or person of vicious habits, irreclaimable by gentle persuasion,' the managers or committee would be entitled with the consent of two-thirds of the members to expel the offender. Such powers would be used but rarely, for 'in a community, where every person is reasonably interested in the industry and good conduct of every other person, idleness and vice will be regarded as indications of idiocy or madness.'

As soon as the first 200 members had paid their deposits, and an equal sum had been subscribed in shares, measures would be taken to commence operations. Subscribers would be called to appoint managers, and land would be rented in the name of trustees appointed by the subscribers. A Treasurer, Thomas Lyons, had already been appointed, and 'to accommodate subscribers' he was taking deposits in weekly instalments. M'Carthy, the Librarian of the Cork Mechanics' Institution, would also receive deposits, and as soon as £50 was collected it would be deposited in the National Provincial Bank.

The *Co-operative Magazine* declared that 'many shares' were already taken and that it watched progress with 'feelings of most sensible pleasure,' for Co-operation would be of especial importance in Ireland, where, 'notwithstanding its great natural resources,' distress and wretchedness abounded. 'Every friend of that long distracted and wretched, though beautiful and naturally much favoured island,' should 'come forward to her rescue and assist in the work of regeneration.'

Despite these enthusiastic phrases, no more was heard of the Cork Community; Frank Podmore, in his *Life of Robert Owen*, is doubtless not far wrong in assuming that, though it served as the prototype for the later ideas of the Co-operators, it never 'advanced beyond the stage of resolutions and paper constitutions.'[11]

15

Practical Directions for Communities

In the late eighteen-twenties Thompson frequently discussed Co-operative tactics at the meetings of the London Co-operators. There, and in a subsequent letter to the *Co-operative Magazine*, he strongly opposed the suggestion that they should abandon the idea of establishing communities in favour of building a Co-operative school. He declared it altogether vain to teach children to love and respect one another if they were immediately treated irrationally and 'surrounded by the hourly example of all the bad passions that afflict humanity and give the lie to the good principles inculcated at school.'[1]

He urged his comrades to sketch out plans for the first community and to convene a meeting to discuss them. Their aim should be to discover the best and quickest method of commencing operations with the smallest number of persons. He followed up this suggestion by himself submitting a plan whereby a mere ten families, with a capital of between £1,200 and £1,500, might set up a Co-operative of twenty-six 'effective labourers.' Once started the size could be increased and further land procured. Families entrusted with the task of heralding in the new social order should be carefully chosen; they should be 'young, well informed married people,' Co-operatively minded and hard-working. On another occasion he sent to the *Co-operative Magazine* a plan for the gardens of Co-operative communities in which the plants, trees, lawns, and artificial lakes would be laid out in the form of a map of the world. He claimed that this would be more 'rational' than the 'childish labyrinth' which George Rapp had taught his 'big children' to construct at the American community of Harmony, for it would stimulate an interest in geography, history, and the manners and habits of nations. Not long afterwards he wrote an essay on the value of water power in the projected communities, in which he praised the technical books issued by the 'Society for the Diffusion of Useful Knowledge.'[2]

In December 1827 he wrote to the *Co-operative Magazine* declaring that the Co-operators were handicapped by lack of information rather than by any shortage of labour or funds; nothing seemed 'more wanting than *practical* directions for the formation of communities.' It was deplorable that no detailed plan had been produced, nor any account of the communitarian ventures at New Harmony and Orbiston as a guide to future builders.

To repair this deficiency he began a work from which many extracts have been given in earlier chapters; under the spur of his fertile imagination and ingenuity it expanded from a planned hundred pages into a book of almost three times that length. This was his last published work, and is entitled *Practical Directions for the Speedy and Economical Establishment of Communities, on the Principles of Mutual Co-operation, United Possessions and Equality of Exertions and of the Means of Enjoyments*. It is dated, Cork, July 1830, and on its title page it bears the inspiring slogan of the Saint-Simonians: 'The age of gold (happiness) which blind credulity has placed in time past, is before us.'

Practical Directions is an amazing work, filled with a thousand and one pieces of information carefully arranged and indexed. There are arguments for Co-operation and against competitive Capitalism; 'practical directions' for communities discussed with infinite care and an almost incredible attention to detail; estimates of the time required to complete each stage of the project, production targets, lists of necessary machinery with their prices and recommended suppliers, monthly instructions for gardening, crop rotation, and other agricultural work; dietary tables showing the comparative value of divers foods, and an examination of the theory and practice of earlier communities with reasons for their success or failure. A wide range of works published in England, France, America, and Prussia is quoted.

In his Introduction he explains that it is his object:

To enable well disposed and intelligent persons to carry the plan of Co-operative industry into effect on the principles laid down so as to make practice correspond with theory.

To provide a fixed plan of operations giving reasons for all details.

To banish random efforts from the future formation of Co-operative Communities.

To enable those undertaking such combinations in different places to understand, correspond with, and aid one another.

To make the establishment of a Co-operative Community as easy as the establishment of any ordinary manufacture, and a much more certainly successful operation.

To show the intelligent and benevolent that, unlike their former lavish expenditure and loss of funds in what from want of knowledge is miscalled charity, they have it in their power, without any sacrifice of funds, and by a *mere temporary loan*, not only to alleviate distress and save their fellow creatures from perishing, but to afford them the means of *permanent independence* and happiness by their own unaided efforts.

Instability or lack of employment, he declared, was 'the master-evil of society as constituted on the principles of *pretended* free competition.' Goods when produced could not be sold at all, or not at a price that would repay the cost of production: therefore manufacturers possessing raw materials and machinery could not give permanent remunerative employment to the 'industrious classes.' The remedy was to find 'an unfailing market for useful produce of all sorts.' Co-operation would accomplish this, 'not by the vain search after foreign markets throughout the globe, no sooner found than overstocked by the restless competition of the starving producers, but by the voluntary union of the industrious classes in such numbers as to afford *a market* to each other.' Such was 'the simple basis of a Co-operative Political Economy,' the first object of which was 'to banish poverty and want from the industrious classes, the great majority of the human race, by giving them unfailing productive employment, in order to rear thereon the structure of social happiness by the subsequent introduction of improvements of all sorts.'[3]

Former attempts at Co-operation had failed through ignorance or lack of funds. They had too often ignored the fact, proved by social experience, that 'equal effort to promote the common good must go hand in hand with equal proprietorship, use and enjoyment.' United possession was 'as superior to the individual possession of competition' as the latter was superior to 'individual possession with slave labour.' The Jesuits in Paraguay and Rapp in North America had 'monopolized the government and the whole possession of what they were pleased to call the common property, keeping the mass of the people in superstitious ignorance and dispensing the products as they thought fit, always reserving to themselves the prophet's share.'[4]

Thompson rejected the suggestions of the *New Harmony Gazette* that Co-operators who were 'easily elated by temporary success and easily depressed by momentary disappointment' should wait until others had 'prepared the way.' Such advice was 'very unlike the promise of an immediate paradise thrown out by Mr Owen.' Nor was anyone justified in asserting that the labour of the children would be sufficient to maintain a community in abundance – love of idleness was a danger which led to the 'self-torment of unoccupied capabilities' as well as to a lack of the 'continual flow of gently pleasureable feelings' which labour produced. Hard work would be needed 'however wisely' affairs were regulated, and no one should condone idleness on the part of either young or old.[5]

The Irish Socialist's plans were framed by the circumstances facing the Co-operators. He declared that those 'who produced everything' were 'utterly destitute of everything' except 'the passing means of existence' which they obtained 'in return for their daily toil.' Yet they had to acquire the means of production. Seizure and gift were 'out of the question'; help from the Government unlikely and undesirable. The only remaining alternatives were loans or 'the small contributions of the industrious classes themselves,' though poverty and lack of education made it improbable that more could be expected from them than 'such small contributions' as would be 'a pledge of their sincere wish to earn their independence.' Subscriptions of one, two, or three pence per head per week in a society of 200 members could be collected, as was being done in Brighton, London, and elsewhere. The alternative was interest-bearing shares of from five to one hundred pounds. Every subscriber of twenty pounds might be given the right of introducing a member into the community. Anyone investing five pounds for himself and fifty shillings for each of his or her children would be admitted.[6]

A minimum average of about twenty pounds per adult and ten pounds per child was required. Two hundred adults would be the smallest nucleus with which it would be prudent to begin, although twice that number would be more useful. The community should be gradually increased to about 2,000.

The first thing to do was to obtain legal security as far as the imperfections of the law would permit. One or more supporters might underwrite the project, but there should always be the possibility of winning full independence by buying out existing proprietors on terms originally agreed upon; this was the 'most essential of the bases of independence and happiness,' and 'the most efficient stimulus' to exertion. The site should allow of adequate room for expansion; people occupying it at the time of its purchase should be invited to join. There should be 'a good stream of water capable of turning a water-wheel, if possible of at least forty horse-power.' The employment of windmills should be considered. There was also the possibility that a new source of energy might be discovered; an economical method of decomposing water, for example, might revolutionize production.

Communities of about 2,000 persons would make the best use of resources. The cost of carriage would be reduced to a minimum; water, central heating, and gas could be economically supplied and an efficient ventilation system operated. Large-scale preparation of meals necessitated a partnership of at least 500 persons; 2,000 could not consume more than half the produce of the smallest flour mill, but two communities might combine to share it. Only a Co-operative of the size proposed could afford sufficient workers to carry out agricultural operations and undertake extensive drainage schemes. Only bodies of a certain size could maintain teachers, physicians, surgeons, chemists, and the like. In a large community it would be possible to find sufficient people of similar interests to develop rich friendships; there would also be more freedom from prying and interference than in tiny villages where the curiosity of persons with few interesting or useful pursuits was directed toward the actions and opinions of their neighbours. Communities should, however, be small enough for members to know each other. More than 2,000 members would be unwieldy; meetings would be difficult to handle, dwellings and workshops would become too far apart, and time would be lost in transporting produce from one part of the community to another.[7]

In a community of 2,000 persons about 1,400 would be of working age. Of these about 600 would produce primary necessities, leaving the remainder free for the production of luxuries. Ninety workers would be engaged in textiles, at least forty in furniture, and 400 in agriculture; thirty would serve as smiths, shoemakers, dressmakers, chemists, and so on. The agriculturalists, with the aid of horses, would cultivate an average of five acres each – a fourth of the normal acreage, as the land would be used intensively.[8]

There could be no return to the pre-industrial way of life. With the aid of machinery a community might become self-sufficient within a year; but it would be 'utterly vain' without it to expect any useful results 'within any reasonable time.' Spinning and weaving equipment could be obtained in either Manchester or Leeds. A spare hundred pounds could not be more judiciously laid out than on an iron works which would afford an occupation for agriculturalists during bad weather. There should be a surplus of machinery for the employment of workers unable to proceed with outdoor work owing to the inclemency of the season.[9]

Some division of labour was essential; 'the very existence of the industrious classes' depended upon it. Owing to the highly specialized character of modern industry, no small community could produce all the commodities it required. Climatic and other geographical differences would also necessitate trade until scientific progress made it possible to produce sugar, tea, nitre, and such articles as cheaply as they could be imported. A patent had been taken out in Berlin for the manufacture of sugar from wheat, but it could probably be obtained 'much more economically from the starch of potatoes,' as was being attempted by Joseph Johnson, an ingenious working chemist in County Cork; extraction from the beet was already meeting with 'much greater success' in France than at the time of Bonaparte's anti-commercial decrees of a couple of decades previously.[10]

Despite all efforts at self-sufficiency, increasing mechanization and the greater incentive of the right to the whole produce of labour might even 'put to shame the boasted exchanges of competition.' Nevertheless, to attain stability the trades to be undertaken needed careful study. No community should export too many essentials, as this would force others to produce non-essentials for exchange, thereby being reduced to 'dependence,' which was one of the evils 'against which it was the object of Co-operation to guard.' Every member should be acquainted with at least one aspect of agricultural work and one industrial process; this would minimize monotony and ensure a high degree of labour mobility.[11]

Labour would be employed much more intensively than in competitive society. Handwork and trenching need no longer be prevented by the number of overseers required. Land wasted by fences between individually owned plots would be utilized; levelling and draining would be conducted on an enlarged scale along scientific lines; liquid manure could be stored in reservoirs and conveyed to the land by long tubes. The tenant's interest in the immediate crop and the landlord's interest in permanent improvement would be unified, and the 'secret or open hostility' between the tenants and labourers over the level of wages would disappear. There would no longer be the incessant problem of searching for the crop which would find an advantageous sale in a market largely unknown.[12]

The first 200 Co-operators could expect an annual yield of 1,960 bushels of grain, 250 tons of potatoes, 60 tons of garden vegetables, 2,500 pounds of flax, 980 bushels of flax seed, and 175 tons of cattle food. This would allow a daily *per capita* consumption in the first year of one-and-a-half pounds of bread, three-and-a-half pounds of potatoes, one-and-a-half pounds of other vegetables, and one pint of milk or its equivalent of dairy produce, a diet which compared well with conditions in competitive society and bettered the recommendations given in the pamphlet *Sure methods of improving health and prolonging life*. On this standard of living they could sell £262 of agricultural produce to meet rent and tithe charges of £275 and create £3,000 of buildings, factories, and other capital goods, and a 'surplus value' of £3,000 in manufactured goods for home use and export.[13]

The communal building should be erected round a square and consist of two storeys and an attic. Architectural details would depend on the taste and resources of the community, and could conform to the 'Gothic, Grecian, Egyptian or barbarian styles,' though simplicity and usefulness' should be the main criteria. A temporary oven and kitchen should first be set up, while tents, sheds, or lodgings in the neighbourhood would furnish temporary accommodation. The top-soil of the area to be built upon should then be removed and transferred to places where the soil was poor. The first building to be erected should house the textile machinery, and should measure one hundred by thirty-six feet. Its lofts and spare rooms would serve as temporary sleeping accommodation. As soon as the masons had completed it they would move on to another while the tilers and carpenters set about their respective trades. Operations should start at the north-east corner of the square and work along from this point, so as to afford shelter from bad weather. At least 200 feet would be completed before the coming of the first winter, when there would already be twenty-four sleeping-rooms and as many sitting-rooms besides one hundred feet of factory buildings and attic space. Each year, a further forty-eight rooms would be added. Soon there would be one sleeping-room and a sitting-room for every adult; sitting rooms should face south or west, bedrooms north or east.[14]

Separate houses on a family basis had originally been countenanced by Co-operative leaders, and had been sympathetically described in Herbert's 'excellent *Visit to the Colony of Harmony in Indiana*'; they had later been rejected because they hindered the emergence of a community spirit, pandered to the despotism of the master of the house, and made woman a domestic drudge. They required an unnecessary duplication of passages, staircases, and cooking and heating arrangements, being 'prescriptions for wasting labour, shortening life and giving rheumatism.' The 'isolated household' must therefore be replaced by the 'communal palace.' It would have four external doors, and only four or five staircases, instead of fifty which would be required under the old system. Ventilation and central heating would be provided by steam or hot-water pipes. Hydraulic pumps would supply piped water on 'the principle of Mr Hague's crane.' Cement floors would be laid along the lines recommended in the *Technical Repository* and approved by William Allen in his pamphlet *Colonies at Home*. The establishment would be lit by gas, which could also be used to flood-light the whole exterior according to the 'very magnificent plan' Owen had proposed. There would be four sets of kitchens and four dining-rooms, one reserved for children. There would also be a mechanical laundry to wash on a large scale, as well as bathrooms with hot water, medical rooms, laboratories, utensil and instrument rooms, libraries, reading-rooms, storerooms, printing-rooms, a book-keeper's office, and a hall for meetings and social gatherings. Children would be housed in attic dormitories until the age of twelve, when they would be allocated individual bedrooms.[15]

The author was not prepared to assent to Owen's claim that clothes were 'largely superfluous' in the English climate and that with a daily bath Communists might dispense with them. Consideration of the question should be deferred until after the community had been established. He also criticized Fourier's idea that workrooms and dormitories should be under one roof remarking that 'noise, dust and effluvia' would pass from the workshops to the domestic apartments. The French writer had nevertheless expressed 'profound views' and made 'many valuable suggestions notwithstanding his extravagancies.'[16]

Thompson was insistent that the assent of all adult members and of 'children capable of forming an opinion' should be obtained before proceeding with the plan or departing from it when agreed upon. 'No person opposed to Co-operative industry should be permitted to manage any department,' however great his or her skill might be. On the other hand, no agreement on 'mere matters of opinion,' either religious or philosophical, should be required; universal freedom of opinion should be the rule. It should ever be borne in mind that man was 'the creature of circumstances'; the 'only effectual way of changing or improving his character and adding to his happiness' was 'by rearranging and improving the circumstances that surround him.'[17]

Practical Directions, like all Thompson's writings, is deeply concerned with the question of education. He declared that since community dwellers would at first be on the verge of penury, there would be neither the time nor the materials for instruction, nor even the places in which to teach. Nevertheless, they had to aim at starting during the first winter when outdoor operations would be curtailed by the weather. 'Profound or learned teachers,' who might indulge a display of learning for the 'gratification of idle personal vanity,' should be avoided in favour of people who would teach 'in the most simple, and therefore the most efficient manner.' Lessons should be utilitarian, but should be of short duration to prevent boredom; there should be frequent visits to interesting places, inspections of machines, walks in gardens, music, dancing, and gymnastic exercises. Rewards and punishments should be avoided, as they fostered competition, caused people to see pleasure in the 'relative inferiority of others,' and directed attention from studies to the trivial questions of good or bad marks. Lectures should be given to young and old alike to explain the general principles of social organization and to contrast Co-operation with the competitive system and the state the community had reached with its 'prospective and ultimate state of independence, improvement and happiness.'[18]

Efforts to Start Communities

Practical Directions caused great excitement in Co-operative circles and among the working class generally. Holyoake likened it to 'a steam-engine, marvellous in the scientific adjustments of its parts' and declared that it was 'precisely' what was needed at a time when 'every step was new and every combination unknown.' The *Poor Man's Advocate* noted with regret that nine out of ten Co-operative societies were 'no more than joint-stock companies,' and began to publish extracts from Thompson's work in the hope that it would diffuse a 'more distinctive' knowledge of Co-operative principles. Thompson's ideas were now everywhere on the upsurge. For almost a decade they had been discussed by Co-operators and socially-conscious workers, and his forceful personality had gradually overcome most of the prejudices which naturally faced so daring and unorthodox a thinker. He had earned a high reputation first as the author of *An Inquiry into the Principles of the Distribution of Wealth*, the most important treatise written by an opponent of the exploitation of labour, and now as the exponent of the only 'scientific' plan for the erection of communities.

His relations with Owen were, however, growing tenuous. In the *Inquiry* he had declared himself neither 'an advocate for or against' the sage of New Lanark,[1] and although the two Co-operative leaders had in subsequent years drawn closer together, there were often minor disagreements between them. Owen, it may be observed, regarded himself as the founder and unchallengeable leader of the Movement and the creator of unique social achievements for the labouring classes. His great manufacturing success and the benefits he had provided at New Lanark had been praised throughout the world. Moreover, he had made immense personal sacrifices. On account of his determination to provide decent conditions for his workers and education for their children he had abandoned his interest in the mills he had created. In his ardour for communities he had lost four-fifths of his fortune at New Harmony. By his attacks on religion and his championship of the rights of the common people he had sacrificed the adulation which had been lavished upon him by royalty and the rich. He therefore considered himself supremely qualified and entitled to guide all future experiments.

William Thompson, on the other hand, was wholly unimpressed by Owen's halo of social success. By temperament a ruthless critic, he was unwilling to refrain from attacking Owen's plans whenever he considered them unsound. He was no respecter of persons, and he was never afraid to criticize either friends or antagonists, though his criticism on the whole was constructive and directed toward the furtherance of Socialist and Co-operative ideals. His experience, moreover, was totally different from that of the hero of New Lanark. He had never operated on the grand scale, nor had he dealt with the large investments of capital employed in cotton manufacture. His was a family of substantial merchants, conducting a relatively static business differing greatly from the mushroom growths of the new mechanized industries, where fortunes were made and lost overnight. He was experienced in the minutiae of farming and trading, and was accustomed to dealing with small margins, with relatively small-scale production and a wide diversity of trade.

His equalitarian and democratic sentiments were affronted by Owen's assumption of authority and contempt for democratic methods. He instinctively distrusted the rich, and could not avoid declaring profound opposition to Owen's claim that capitalists could or should be induced to provide the means to establish Co-operative projects. Nor could he share Owen's belief that the governing classes, so firmly devoted to the preservation of their own privileges, would assist the Co-operative cause.

Practical Directions and Thompson's other writings placed him, rather than Owen, in the forefront of the Movement. Moreover, his call to commence immediate operations brought the two protagonists into scarcely concealed conflict, for Owen, after his bitter experience at New Harmony, was reluctant to proceed with a new attempt. Under such circumstances the relations between the two leaders were of vital importance; upon them depended the unity of the Movement and the direction in which it would move. On March 18, 1830, the Irishman wrote to Owen from 105, Grafton Street, Dublin, begging him to realize that advocacy of immediate community building need not conflict with other articles of the Owenite programme. The letter was conciliatory and couched in terms of respect and friendship:

I am looking out with hope and pleasure for your development of intermediate arrangement with the aid of political power to introduce our views gradually. While you are boldly operating on the whole mass, I am endeavouring to arrange a little part of the social machine, not forgetting its connections with the whole.[2]

The correspondence which followed is not extant. We may infer, however, that Owen was not mollified, for the *Co-operative Magazine*, which he now controlled, ignored Thompson's community plans.

To break Owen's Press stranglehold William Pare founded a *Magazine of Useful Knowledge and Co-operative Miscellany*, and William Carpenter his *Political Letters and Pamphlets*. Both these journals discussed economic problems along Thompsonian lines, and published news of his plans to begin community building. They went further in political controversy than even the old *Co-operative Magazine* had done, demanding an untaxed Press and the enfranchisement of the working class which Thompson had championed in *Labour Rewarded*.

Carpenter's periodical was deeply interested in Thompson's community plans. The first issue, dated January 1831, advertised *Practical Directions* and announced a meeting in the London Mechanics' Institute, where the Editor would discuss the failure of past communities and the conclusions to be drawn therefrom. A page of Co-operative news by William Lovett, the secretary of the British Association for the Promotion of Co-operative Knowledge, was instituted which became a regular feature. The April issue carried a letter from Reynolds, a leading Co-operator of the First Birmingham Society, urging that *Practical Directions* should be 'the guide to work by.' In the following issue James Tucker responded: 'The proposal of the first Birmingham Society to form a community on Mr Thompson's Practical System should be taken into immediate consideration by every society in the kingdom.' Everyone should use his 'utmost endeavour to promote it.' Hitherto Co-operators had intended to employ their members in manufacturing to make them 'independent,' but this was difficult on account of lack of funds. Thompson's plan, however, would allow resources to be pooled and operations carried out on a 'large scale'; Communism would be advanced from an ultimate ideal to an 'immediate' possibility. Arrangements should not be under the direction of community members, but solely under the superintendence of 'Mr Thompson himself,' who alone possessed a 'thorough knowledge of the principles of the system.' Co-operative societies should 'prevail on him to undertake the organization,' and agree to 'take no part in its direction' but to 'obey him,' for he alone was competent.

To implement these proposals, the ensuing issue of *Political Letters and Pamphlets* announced that a national congress of Co-operative societies would be held in Manchester on May 26 and 27. 'Several eminent and zealous advocates of the cause, including Robert Owen, William Thompson, Minter Morgan, Dr MacCormac, William Pare of Birmingham, John Finch of Liverpool, and Eaton of Huddersfield' would be present; and it was hoped that the union of Co-operators might achieve for the whole human race what 'Catholic Association' had achieved for the Emerald Isle.

As soon as the delegates arrived it was evident that the Movement had entered a new and enthusiastic phase. Forty-four societies were represented by delegates, some of whom had travelled hundreds of miles; many sympathizers attended in their private capacities, while societies unable to afford delegates' expenses sent messages of support. The Manchester Association for the spread of Co-operative Knowledge welcomed the delegates and arranged that the gathering was well attended by local working men.

Everyone insisted that Co-operative trading schemes were no more than 'stepping stones to communities of mutual co-operation,' and that all efforts should be directed towards the establishment of a community as Thompson had directed. Two hundred member societies were called upon each to elect one member and supply thirty pounds in order that a community of 200 persons might immediately be formed with a capital of £6,000. Thompson moved and Owen seconded a resolution that all moneys should be sent to John Dixon, the President of the North-west of England United Co-operative Company, at the *Courant* office in Chester, and that he should call a meeting as soon as the shares had been subscribed. Owen and Thompson were both included among the trustees entrusted with founding the community, and the latter's influence was evident from the fact that the committee included his close friends, Pare, Finch, and MacCormac.[3]

Thompson announced that his land at Carhoogariff, about 600 acres well supplied with water, peat, and timber, was being held in readiness for the Co-operators should they desire it. He would make it available for a low rent, on perpetual lease, and with power to make a twenty years' purchase on the basis of the rent originally agreed upon. He would himself pay the membership contribution and join the first community, whether it were established on his own land or elsewhere; he would give all the advice and assistance in his power, but wished for no more privileges than any other member.[4] Some time earlier, in a letter to the *Co-operative Magazine*, he had offered to present his estate at Carhoogariff to the Co-operative Trading Fund Association outright if it would take up his project and carry it to fruition.

After the Congress Thompson stayed on in Manchester to address the Mechanics' Institution under the auspices of the *Voice of the People*, the organ of the National Association for the Protection of Labour.[5] Between 200 and 250 persons were present, most of them factory workers who paid threepence for a seat in the arena or a penny in the gallery. The speaker was indisposed, his voice feeble; nevertheless, his enthusiasm spurred him to speak for two hours, and he continued answering eager questions from his audience for another hour and twenty minutes before the meeting was finally adjourned.

He began by relating that Robert Owen had addressed himself to the rich and had obtained publicity by paying at advertisement rates for the insertion of his writings in *The Times* and other newspapers, but with little success, for the rich were not interested in his schemes. Though he had accumulated an ample fortune at New Lanark, he had sold his shares in that project because his partners, Jeremy Bentham, 'the celebrated writer in legislation,' Allen, 'the famous Quaker,' and others, did not agree with plans for giving a 'finished education' to his employees. The response of the working class had been quite different. William Bryan, a Brighton workman, believing that Owen's plan might serve if small subscriptions were made by working people to establish trading societies, had found a number of men to support his plan, which was working well.

Saint-Simon, who had fought for American independence in company with Lafayette, had returned home with ideas very like those of Owen. He advocated universal education and the abolition of inheritance in rank and property. Himself a rich man, he had urged his opinions on high society and on the *literati*, but with little success. He spent his fortune and died in poverty in 1825. After his death, however, a group of 'spirited young men' had begun to hold weekly meetings in Paris to develop and propagate his principles; they had attracted considerable attention, and were becoming stronger every day; already they had the finest 'temple' in Paris, a regular newspaper, and 'missionaries' who travelled throughout France. They contended that all property should be given to the Government and everyone rewarded according to his services to the State. There was, of course, no landed aristocracy in France, for the Revolution had swept it away, but there was a moneyed aristocracy which, if not prevented, would produce as much misery as the aristocrats had done.

Co-operative ideas were everywhere on the upsurge; even in America they were making rapid progress, for Skidmore had 'published largely' on the subjects and had devised plans for carrying it into effect.

Co-operation was advocated with the greatest mildness, for everyone would ultimately benefit by it. The rich were hostile, some considering the idea wild, others immoral; but Co-operators pitied them for their ignorance and desired to explain that no one was asked to give up even one of his bawbees without receiving more in return. It was difficult, however, to get these ideas across, as the Press was hostile.

The rich claimed that Co-operation had failed even under such good managers as Owen, Hamilton, and Combe. It was necessary frankly to examine the cause of past failures. Owen had failed at New Harmony because he had not made the land available to the members. The first two or three years were necessarily the most laborious; great incentives were therefore needed – the best stimulus was to possess the land. This had not been understood either at Orbiston or New Harmony. Owen said he had given the colonists the land – 'but how? Why, by reserving so much of the produce to himself and his trustees that the people thought themselves worse off than in the old society.' At Orbiston 3,000 acres of good land had been taken at a rent of four pounds an acre and interest had to be paid on £10,000. So little attention had been paid to the selection of members that one arrived from London who could do nothing but gild picture-frames and make looking-glasses! Abram Combe, the organizer, lacked energy; he had been unable to face the 'base opposition' of selfish persons who wanted to wrench the government from his hands. His weakness had led to a struggle by individuals to get what they could. At New Harmony, which Owen had purchased at a cost of £40,000, backwoodsmen had similarly been gathered together without selection. The members were so little trusted that a guard was stationed at the orchards to preserve them from depredations. As Owen had 'in great measure admitted,' sharp-witted Americans had obtained two-thirds of his property by fraud. After a year's absence he had returned to find the community so inextricably involved in debt that it had to be abandoned. Owen had said that though the colony was a failure in the eyes of the general public, it was no failure to him, because he had foreseen the collapse, and the experience he had gained was worth it all. Thompson, for his part, would no more be concerned in a community for which he could foresee the ruin of those involved in it than he would voluntarily cease to live. Nevertheless, initial defeats were not surprising; the 'grand plan' of Co-operation, like any other new project, could not be expected to succeed without some losses. Co-operators should persevere. As soon as the first community was established they would be able to say, 'Come and see how we possess and enjoy more real wealth and happiness than a fortune of £100,000 could give to any individual.' By the peaceful process of buying up the land bit by bit, the whole country would become the property of the people. Pauperism would be annihilated without the employment of a government agency as was required by the Saint-Simonian plan. Each district would act for itself under the broad co-ordination of general laws; the whole world would ultimately merge into one Co-operative union, where there would be no individually owned property but perfect equality.

There were a great number of men ready to carry the plan forward. This had not been the case when Owen in England and others in France had first called public attention to their ideas. Limited schemes of Co-operation were now in existence which pointed the way for future progress, even if in themselves open to grave criticism. The dyers near Manchester, for example, had formed a Co-operative to provide work for their unemployed. A recent visit to this establishment had shown him that it possessed many weaknesses. Employment was given at an expense of nearly £3,000, or forty pounds per head; the lease would expire in twenty-one years, when the greater part of the capital would be lost; the establishment was only equipped to employ up to seventy persons; moreover, so little foresight had been exercised in selecting the site that only thirty-five workers could be employed on account of water shortage; there was no opening for further hands when a 'turn-out' occurred. Communities would be preferable as instruments for giving work to the unemployed; they would provide permanent employment and a greater variety of work.

Thompson exhibited two plans for the proposed communities, one prepared by himself, the other by Robert Owen. The principal difference between them was that under Owen's scheme members would live in separate houses, while in his the entire community would dwell in a single building. Owen had told him his plan was 'very erroneous,' but when asked to specify his objections he had replied he had 'not time.' Thompson concluded his address by declaring that both Owen and he would be very happy to hear any objection to their respective plans, and would be 'highly gratified' to see anybody carry into operation the 'great principles' for which they had both written largely and laboured much. For his own part he did not consider he knew everything. Dr Tucker at this point once again declared the Irishman the fittest person to have 'entire control,' but Thompson replied no one should have other than delegated power, removable at the will of the constituent body. If there were any dictatorship the community must come to ruin. In answer to a question by E. T. Craig, the manager of the Irish Co-operative of Ralahine, he declared that twenty pounds per adult should suffice to establish a community of 200 persons in Ireland; while in England thirty pounds for every adult, and half that sum for every child under fifteen, would be needed. A long and 'very animated' discussion followed, in which Craig, Elijah Dixon, and the Manchester trade-union leader, John Doherty, participated before an adjournment was agreed on.

At the resumed lecture the number of the audience was well maintained; though there was an entrance fee of twopence, some sixty persons assembled at eight o'clock, an hour fixed 'to accommodate the operatives,' and the number grew to upwards of 150. The lecturer explained that his purpose was to afford opportunity for further discussion. He described the structure of his proposed community house in detail, claiming that it was shaped to secure the privacy of the interior gardens and to enclose the greatest area of land for a given length of building. The structure should be on high land in the centre of the community farm; manure laid there would be automatically washed down by the rain into the lower fields.

Elijah Dixon asked how it would be possible to induce the English 'so tenacious of their privacy' to live in intimacy with their neighbours. (This was a question by which Co-operators were often troubled.) Thompson replied that all proper privacy would be afforded, but that it would not be right 'to afford to villainy any shelter at all'; the dissipated and the tyrannical were always the first to call for secrecy. So far from being like a barracks, where a crowd of men saw each other undress and all slept in the same room, every adult would have two rooms twelve feet square. Someone interjected that people liked to have houses at a distance from one another to avoid having their affairs known. The Irishman answered that under competition the chief reason why people wanted separate dwellings was to keep their schemes secret from their rivals; in a community such a motive would not exist.

Johnson argued that sleeping in separate houses prevented the summoning of medical aid in case of urgency. The speaker agreed; the King himself did not always keep his physician at Windsor; and the poor had to accept what accident or charity threw in their way. In a community a medical man would dwell on the premises; he could be called within three minutes, and would be able to observe his patients from day-to-day familiarity. The doctor in competitive society benefited from the existence of diseases, and was concerned with curing rather than preventing illness; in a community he would be interested in keeping everyone in good health. A member of the audience complained that Owen's medical baths had been ignored; Thompson replied that adequate plans for baths would certainly be made, but in the existing state of knowledge little more could be done than afford room for their subsequent erection.

J. A. Smith, a member of the Royal College of Surgeons, 'agreed with the lecturer'; he eulogized the health provisions of France under Napoleon and the establishment of a French Ministry of Public Health, regretting there was no such Ministry in Britain. He regarded medicated baths as 'medicated humbug.'

In reply to another question Thompson declared little was yet known of the best diet to sustain health; communities would afford ideal conditions for all investigations concerning 'the science of human society.' (Someone here interjected that the Irish, who subsisted on potatoes, were a hardy race, to which an Irishman in the audience retorted that it was 'not the potatoes which made the Irish live, but a miracle.' If they had good roast beef they would live longer – a remark which was greeted with cheers and laughter.)

To the question 'What provision would be made for the proper observance of the Sabbath?' Thompson replied that community members would be subject to the general laws of the land, and would be under no great temptation to break them than other people. Labour-saving devices might make it possible for Wednesday, as well as Sunday, to be a day of rest. (Great applause.)

Lengthy reports of the lectures were published in the Manchester Press. The *Guardian* was hostile, but admitted that though 'some few' of the audience may have been 'induced to attend from curiosity,' the majority were sympathizers. The *Manchester Times and Gazette* was more sympathetic, declaring that Thompson had 'successfully answered several very pointed objections' and had been heard 'with the greatest attention and a very uncommon degree of interest.' *Wheeler's Manchester Chronicle* defended the old order against Thompson's egalitarian views, complaining that in the world he advocated 'the clearer of the muck-midden, the judge, and the manager of public affairs would receive the same description of education, be entitled to the same rank and enjoy an equal share of the good things produced either by the manure of the first, the judicial qualities of the second, or the 'management' of the last!'

A second Co-operative congress was held in the autumn of the same year in Birmingham, where Pare had done much propaganda. The sessions continued for three days, commencing October 4. Thompson once again played a leading role, making suggestions how best to develop Co-operative propaganda as well as on the question of the establishment of communities. He was now referred to as the delegate of a Cork Co-operative Society with offices at 14, The Parade, Cork.[6]

On the first day of the Congress he proposed that 'Co-operative Missionaries' should travel the length and breadth of the country on the Saint-Simonian pattern to proclaim the Co-operative gospel and to assist with the forming of local branches. Observing that some Co-operators regarded trading as the main objective, while others 'very properly' did not consider this Co-operation at all, he urged that 'missionaries' be forbidden to preach conflicting doctrines, and proposed that Owen, Minter Morgan, John Gray, and himself should present a copy of their works to the 'missionaries' and that no doctrine not common to all should be preached. The London Committee should meanwhile draw up a definitive Code of Instructions.

The Rev Marriott, a delegate from Warrington, declared that almost all the Co-operation he knew had been learnt from Owen or from Thompson, whose *Inquiry* was 'as far superior to Smith's *Wealth of Nations* as one book can be to another' – a remark which was greeted by 'immediate applause.' Nevertheless, he complained, both propagandists made anti-religious observations which not all Co-operators accepted, and which might be used by enemies in attacking the Movement. Thompson's proposal, however, was accepted by general consent, because it served to exclude personal vagaries without necessarily pledging the Movement to atheism. Thompson proposed that the missionaries should be paid twopence a mile for travelling, plus a shilling a day board, on the ground that they should not make a profit out of working men. He declared 'he enjoyed as much pleasure in eating, drinking, and travelling as any man, and it cost him no more.' Other delegates, however, considered the proposals too meagre and a reflection of the proposer's own unusually economical habits; it was therefore agreed that hospitality should be received from the various societies.

On the second day of the Congress discussion of community building began. The project again received enthusiastic support. Benjamin Warden 'felt an inward consciousness of the practicability of forming a community'; he declared that he had 'no other expectation for his old age than to be sent to a workhouse unless a community were established'; the four London societies he represented 'would not be satisfied with his spending their money in coming to the Congress' unless he could show progress on his return. If they were active 'they might almost get into community before the next Congress,' which was to be held the following spring. Gill of Kendal asked what would happen if a minority in a society wished to join a community but were opposed by an unwilling majority; T. Cook replied that propaganda and the success of the first community would educate all Co-operators, and that community-building would win the friendship of the middle class, whereas trading only provoked the opposition of private traders – 'the establishment of one community would do more good than a hundred thousand grocers' shops.' Thompson joined in, himself offering to pay the entry fee of anyone unable to enter community; he hoped that others would induce their well-to-do friends to follow suit.

Owen was carried away by the occasion, flamboyantly declaring that communities such as he recommended had never failed because they had never been attempted. There was a science of society, as certainly as a science of mathematics, but it was as yet unknown. With one-hundredth of the land and capital, he could provide a better system than that existing. It was the duty of Governments to assist Co-operation, not to make wars. Public opinion was ready to force the Government to realize that the means of banishing poverty were known; in future every child might become 'a good, a virtuous and a charitable being.'

The Rev Marriott spoke of the significance of the doctrine of necessity and complained that the Government, the laws, the Press, and the education system were all inimical to new ideas. He had been delighted with the 'admirable observations' on that point in Thompson's *Inquiry* and hoped to elaborate the theme 'at no distant day.'[7]

As a result of the discussion it was agreed to revise the decision of the last Congress confiding the establishment of the projected community to the trustees of the North-west of England United Co-operative Company, who seem to have done nothing. A special committee was now elected to take over the job. Its members included Thompson, Owen, Warden, Marriott, MacCormac, Doherty, Hamilton, and Vandeleur. They were charged with the 'immediate formation of a community' and were to draw up 'a Prospectus of the Objects and Nature of a Community upon a Social System.'

On the last day Thompson was elected chairman of the Congress and was re-elected representative of Cork in the North-west of England Co-operative Company. He seconded a resolution recommending subsidies for two Co-operative journals, one of which was *The Voice of the People*, under whose auspices he had spoken at Manchester. Later he joined Warden and Powell in opposing what they regarded as an unnecessary vote of thanks to Robert Owen. It was not put, but, as the Irish Socialist remarked, was 'passed without the ceremony of voting.' Unimportant in itself, this incident was but a prelude to later developments and evidence that there was already a reaction against adulation of Owen and submission to his authoritarian leadership. Great enthusiasm was, however, aroused by the Congress, which was immediately followed by meetings in many parts of the country. 'Mr Thompson of Cork' was kept busy addressing them; at one of the most important, held in the metropolis, he spoke with Owen and Trench.

A third Co-operative Congress met in London on April 23, 1832, at the Co-operative Institution in Gray's Inn Road. Delegates representing sixty-five societies and 800 observers assembled in the expectation of hearing that practical steps had at last been taken by the committee appointed in the previous year. In everyone's mind, observes William Lovett, was the project 'of forming an incipient community upon the plan of Mr Thompson of Cork.'[8]

The enthusiasm of the rank and file, however, soon became affected by a tense atmosphere which emanated from the committee. Rumours circulated that Owen, in defiance of the committee charged with this task, had altered the circular addressed to Members of Parliament. Lovett, who was a member of the committee, records that when he and his colleagues waited on the sage of New Lanark to protest to him, he had answered 'with the greatest composure' that his action was 'evidently despotic,' but that since the Co-operators were 'all ignorant of his plans and of the objects he had in view' they must 'consent to be ruled by despots' till they 'had acquired sufficient knowledge' to govern themselves. 'After such vainglorious avowal,' comments Lovett, 'what could we say but report – in the phraseology of one of the deputation – that we had been flabbergasted?'

Before the report of the committee was reached, the first skirmishes between Owen and Thompson occurred. The anti-capitalist writer, John Gray, was bitterly attacked by Owen, who complained that Gray had not read his (Owen's) works with attention and did not understand the questions at issue. Thompson defended his fellow theoretician, declaring he saw no reason to assume that Gray had not studied the master's works; for his own part he had studied them fully and considered Owen's labour-exchange banks impracticable. Not long afterwards, with the support of Pare, he forced a discussion on Owen's *Address to the Governments of Europe and America*, which he declared too vague. He observed with sarcasm that Governments were told the Co-operative system possessed all wisdom, but that if they desired to know anything at all about it 'they must address themselves to the Co-operative headquarters in Gray's Inn Road.' He succeeded in getting the manifesto passed to a committee for re-wording. He also countered praise of Owen's Co-operative school in America by acidly inquiring whether the teachers were paid out of profit or capital. Warden joined in the criticism, declaring Owen's projects too despotic.[9]

When Owen rose to speak it was evident that in the last few months he had grown extremely cool towards community building. He dwelt on the need for support from the Government, and to the general surprise he urged that 'those who had minds to reflect – and did reflect – must be aware' that the establishment of small communities such as Thompson suggested was not in the interests of the Movement. It was 'much easier' to establish things on a grander scale; Co-operators should 'come forward in a body' and 'compel the adoption of their system' by the Government 'complete and well organized in all its parts.' Thompson at once replied that he could not see how to 'set about calling upon the Government to adopt the measures which the Co-operative Societies had in view.' Societies should not relax their efforts, but should exert themselves to the full.

When the report of the committee was reached it was urged that, owing to the violent disagreement which had developed, the Press should be excluded. Tempers rose high; 'it was not wise,' reports Lovett, 'to embody much of the discussion in the official report of the proceeding.'

The situation was indeed grim. The committee reported 'with regret' that as a result of the differences among the Co-operators only two societies had replied to their offer of shares. No money had been received except from Pare's First Birmingham Society, and that merely a deposit of six pounds on two shares. Many societies were utilizing the whole of their meagre funds for trading; others to start the North-west of England Co-operative Society, considering it 'better calculated for the present to advance their interests.' This disappointing report was in itself sufficient to depress the most buoyant Co-operator. To make matters worse, it had been found that the policies of the two foremost Co-operative leaders were in complete conflict; their personal relations had become deeply embittered.

The strife that had been waged in the committee now broke forth in open Congress. Thompson opened with a fierce attack. Together with one of the two other members of the committee not resident in London he had journeyed there 'for the purpose of beginning practical operations,' and had insisted on a circular being drawn up and sent to the societies in accordance with the instructions of the last Congress. Owen, however, had affronted them with the demand that they should abandon the attempt and form themselves into a committee for 'universal correspondence,' which he wrongly alleged was the object for which they had been appointed. He had 'startled the committee' by declaring he would not consent to his name being associated with any attempt to establish a community with less than £240,000, and had then withdrawn from the committee 'paralysing its exertions.' The Irish Socialist protested that he had himself always been willing to collaborate with his fellow members, and appealed for the appointment of a new committee of 'practical men.'

Styles, Austin, and Warden, all of whom had served on the committee, sided with Thompson. They declared that inaction had not arisen from any negligence or apathy on their part. Pare declared there was enough support for the immediate establishment of a community and repeated his proposal, which had been agreed to at the previous Congress, that a detailed prospectus be circulated. He was echoed by Lovett, who argued that the 'happy state of society promised by Mr Owen' could be realized only 'through the medium of incipient communities.' The Rev Marriott was warmly applauded when he gave a pledge to quit his profession and enter the first community. At this point Owen entered the debate, declaring that nothing he had heard proposed had a chance of success. The question at issue was whether or not communities were to be independent of the outside world. They should be independent; therefore they could not be small. Moreover, it was doubtful whether small communities could compete with capitalist production. It would be easier and quicker to build a large community than a small one, and would give much greater satisfaction. It was untrue to say that communities had failed at New Lanark, New Harmony, and Orbiston, as these experiments had never been communities; their members had refused to follow his policy and had wasted all their time talking. Had people followed him when he had come forward in 1817 'the world by this time would have been a perfect paradise.' He announced that a friend had offered 420 acres of good tithe-free land, within seventeen miles of London, at twenty-two shillings and sixpence an acre. Adjacent land was available for subsequent extension, and the situation was admirable. This offer should be accepted. While advocating this purchase and thereby apparently giving some approval to the view that the Co-operators could initiate a community, he proceeded to repeat the suggestion that such action was unnecessary because the Government understood the virtue of communities and only awaited the maturity of public opinion 'to effect those happy changes which Co-operation was adapted to realize.'

Despite Owen's speech, which seemed an effort to postpone community building to a vague and remote future, Lovett, Pare, and Styles moved a resolution calling for 'redoubled exertions.' Lovett insisted on the need to free the industrious classes from 'the devastating and irritating influence of the competitive system' and repudiated the view that the Government would help them. Pare declared that Owen had 'not only too highly estimated the contingent results of his own proceedings in opening the purses of the affluent,' but 'too meanly estimated the capabilities and powers of the labouring classes.' Finch and some seven other Co-operators expressed similar views, while Wigg of Kingsland defended the Orbiston experiment against Owen's criticism. Only Nash of Sheffield and Flather of the Western Union thought that Co-operators lacked the knowledge and good feeling necessary to fit themselves for the task, but Warden, another Western Union delegate, retorted that they would not improve while in 'the present wretched state of society.'

Owen then wound up the first half of the discussion. 'What wisdom,' he asked, 'would there be in taking a savage from the wilds of America who could not tell the difference between the numbers five and ten, and placing him in Cambridge University to teach the professor mathematics?' Community building must be founded on practical methods and placed in the hands of practical people. He himself had been experimenting for forty years. The question was whether to follow 'Mr Thompson's plan' by attempting a community with £6,000 or to adopt his own counsel. He had 'the greatest possible esteem for Mr Thompson,' but 'begged leave to assure him that he knew little of this matter.' Even £60,000 would be of little avail, but if they were 'united as *one man* and fully determined to prosecute their plan,' many on the Stock Exchange would be willing to advance capital. Money lenders were favourable to Co-operation when they found it practicable; if an 'intelligible and satisfactory statement' were put before them, they would advance 'almost any amount at 4 per cent.' He was 'glad to see the meeting so impatient to proceed'; but they should put their impatience to some purpose by 'losing no time in making proposals to moneyed men.'

Lovett has recorded the subsequently highly controversial proceedings which are omitted from the published report:

We retired for dinner; when we came back, our friend Owen told us very solemnly in the course of a long speech, that if we were resolved to go into a community upon Mr Thompson's plan, we must make up our minds *to dissolve our present marriage connections, and go into it as single men and women.* This was like the burst of a bombshell in the midst of us. One Co-operator after another, who had been ardently anxious for this proposal of a community, began to express doubts, or flatly to declare that he would never consent to it, while others considered that living in the community need not interfere in any way with marriage. One poor fellow, Mr Petrie, an enthusiast in his way, quite agreed with his brother Owen, but made a speech which many blushed to hear contending that it would make no difference as far as he and his wife were concerned, for she would follow him anywhere.

'Nothing,' commented Lovett, 'could have been better devised than the speech of Mr Owen to sow seeds of doubt and to cause the scheme to be abortive.' Yet despite Owen's bombshell, Carson of Birkacre spoke eloquently in support of Thompsonite communities. Many people in Lancashire, he claimed, seriously intended forming such a community. The Worsley Co-operators could obtain uncultivated land at one pound per acre; at Liverpool 1,000 acres of land were available, and labour only was needed; in a few years the plan would lead to the formation of a valuable estate. 'After reading the works of Messrs Owen and Thompson, the people were anxious to commence a community.' Hirst of Shipley also spoke in support of communities, but a clergyman, the 'Rev Dunn of Lindley', sided with Owen.

Thompson returned to the fray. He declared it necessary to distinguish between communities which would create a 'state of bliss' and those that were 'a kind of superior workhouse or workshops for the poor.' Amid laughter he declared that with sufficient capital and 2,000 individuals he did not despair of showing the world an institution which would 'even please Mr Owen,' but he did not agree that the security the Co-operators could offer would be satisfactory to money lenders. If a first-rate community could not be built at once, it was necessary to start on a smaller scale. Even in the sandy soil of Holland the condition of the poor had been greatly alleviated by Co-operative methods; Englishmen would indeed be stupid if they could not achieve similar results. At Mr Vandeleur's Irish community at Ralahine much had been done with little capital. The difficulty of getting ignorant people to work without personal incentive had been understood. Everyone had been taught to understand that if one or two people stopped working the produce of the community would be reduced. Public opinion had caused every member to exert himself. A committee of members met each evening to determine the work for the ensuing day, and there were no idlers.[10]

Owen here interjected that experience had taught him that 'committees and majorities would never answer' – 'a head was needed.' He had himself the necessary experience to direct the affairs of a community, and had no objection to making another experiment. On Lovett's protesting against such advocacy of absolute government, Owen replied that 'no one was more opposed to despotism' than he, whereat Thompson asked with sarcasm whether 'Mr Owen had taken care to give to the world after his death the valuable knowledge he possessed.'

At length, despite Owen's vehement opposition, the resolution to proceed with Thompson's plan was carried. Thompson, Pare, and Wigg were entrusted with the task of drawing up a prospectus. Thompson also obtained assent for a motion that as soon as a hundred shares were subscribed at least 400 acres of land should be obtained. Together with Hoskins, Bromley, and Hamilton, he was appointed a trustee to make the purchase.

After this strenuous discussion optimism was partly restored by the progress reports of some hundreds of Co-operative trading societies. These showed a considerable growth in funds accumulated by weekly threepenny and sixpenny contributions. In a number of areas productive Co-operatives had been established; 'beautiful specimens of woollens, linens, hats, shoes, stockings and hardware of almost every description' were being manufactured.

Owen and Thompson both declared that no religious sectarianism was implied by Co-operation, the latter significantly adding it was 'not necessary to adopt all Mr Owen's tenets in order to co-operate with him.' The rival leaders were then appointed with Bromley to inspect the estate at Aylesbury which Owen thought suitable for a community. Towards the close of the proceedings Thompson was once more voted to the chair. He again played a prominent part, this time with Owen's support, in urging that the 'missionaries' should preach a codified body of doctrine. He was entrusted with supervising the 'missionaries' in Dublin and Cork, two of the nine districts into which the British Isles were divided for Co-operative purposes. On a motion of Pare and Benbow he was also appointed to a committee to inquire into the work of the North-west of England Co-operative Trading Company.

The Co-operators sought to gloss over the differences between their two leaders; nevertheless, Lovett remarks, 'When we retired Mr Thompson expressed himself very strongly against Owen's conduct.' The Irish Socialist had, however, scored a remarkable victory. The Co-operators had rallied to his plan and rejected the arguments of the world-famous pioneer of New Lanark who had gained the ear of Governments and Crowned Heads. Thompson's success may be attributed in part to his democratic methods and opinions, which contrasted with his rival's baldly expressed desire for personal autocracy, and in part to his lucidity in debate and the influence which he had gained by his writings. He had behind him a body of ardent and convinced disciples. Moreover, he had laid before the Congress a concrete proposal for social amelioration which in view of its modest scale and its apparent chance of speedy fruition made a strong appeal both to the poverty and to the ardour of the Movement.

The national Press hardly noticed the Congress, and even the Co-operative journals gave rather meagre reports, despite the fact that three Members of Parliament were present. Owen's *Crisis*, not unnaturally, avoided too many disclosures. The rank and file therefore learnt little of Owen's 'bombshell' or of the conflict between the two foremost protagonists. *Table Talk*, a Co-operative tract which appeared in

Birmingham in 1832, referred to the eminence of the two leaders 'whose ardent wishes and ceaseless exertions' were 'above all praise.' It declared that Thompson had made out his case and that the result of the Congress 'would be the outfitting at once of a community on Thompson's plan.' The *Lancashire and Yorkshire Co-operator* spoke for the mass of the Movement when it proclaimed that 'happiness could alone be secured in Co-operative Villages or Communities on the plan of W. Thompson.' The movement was growing rapidly: the *Monthly Repositor*, impressed by the fact that 'delegates from associated bodies travelled hundreds of miles bringing voices from the four winds to meet in grave congress and to report the actual existence of several hundreds of Co-operative societies,' remarked that it began 'almost to doubt the propriety of hinting or paragraphing off the question of Co-operation any longer.'

Nevertheless, when the fourth Co-operative Congress met in Liverpool at the beginning of October neither Owen nor Thompson were present – the latter perhaps being prevented from attending by illness. The atmosphere was deflated, and the number of delegates considerably smaller than at former congresses. The community project had not advanced much since their earlier gathering, though most of the speakers continued to declare its establishment their principal object. Pare begged the delegates to direct their attention to that part of Thompson's *Practical Directions* which treated of the numbers necessary to commence a community. Its author had 'shown pretty clearly' that it would be 'indiscreet' to commence with less than 200 and that they must be selected on a basis of skill and enthusiasm.

The general feeling was characterized by a delegate who said that Co-operators were mostly so poor that when they learned thirty pounds per head would be required to establish a community they 'almost despaired of its accomplishment in their day'; self-confidence gave way in some quarters to a childish hope that a rich capitalist would assist them; others reflected that 'they had children who would reap the benefit of their exertions if they themselves could not.' But though optimism was damped, it was decided to persevere; Thompson's belief in a small community still held the field. With virtual unanimity it was agreed to support his plan, and it was to his *Practical Directions* that the chairman and others turned in discussing the details of the project.[11]

Its author, however, was now a dying man. He seems to have realized that efforts to establish a community were proving inconclusive. The

Co-operators had been reluctant to accept his offer to begin work on his estate, declaring that a start should be made in England, if possible near London; but divided counsels, lack of financial resources, and preference for trading held back progress.

Nevertheless, the horizon was not entirely dismal. Many eyes turned to the Ralahine Co-operative, which had been established by John Scott Vandeleur in 1830 and had become a Mecca for social reformers. Vandeleur, a convert to Owenism and the owner of an estate of 618 acres, had caused his tenants to cultivate it on a Co-operative basis, although as landlord and capitalist he continued to draw both rent and interest. Under the administration of E. T. Craig the establishment led a prosperous existence until the proprietor brought about its collapse in 1833 through his fatal addiction to gambling. Thompson was warmly appreciative of the experiment. Craig, who was impressed by the 'practical turn' of his mind, records that when the Irish Socialist visited Ralahine he presented him with a copy of his *Practical Directions* and declared that what he saw strengthened a determination he had long held of proceeding on 'somewhat similar lines' at Glandore.[12]

It was not surprising that William Thompson should have returned to his cherished scheme of establishing a community on his own estate. His labours as a Socialist and Co-operative theorist had in no way caused him to lose interest in his tenants, among whose descendants memories of his generous personality have lived on for more than a century. From researches made in the locality it appears that he began work in the 'townland' of Carhoogariff and constructed a round tower a hundred feet high on a lofty peak overlooking the estate.[13] This he furnished as a private residence and the centre of operations. Local tradition claims that from its windows he watched the sails of the ships advancing towards the busy port which he planned to develop, and directed the construction of a row of buildings which probably were to form one side of the community he never lived to finish.

17

A Bequest to the Co-operative Movement

Never robust, Thompson had been suffering for several years from a chest affliction which he was aware might at any time prove fatal. After a violent paroxysm of coughing he would say playfully, 'Ah! If only I could live for ever, be for ever young, active, joyous, and useful; but as it is, I must make the best of a short life.'

In the spring of 1833, though bedridden and medically advised that his death could not be long delayed, his interest in Co-operative affairs was undimmed. He continued his correspondence with Co-operative friends and, on March 14, he wrote from Rosscarbery to E. T. Craig of Ralahine asking for news of the Movement and stating that he could not 'say whether death would arrive in three days, three weeks, or three months.' His end came only fourteen days later, on March 28. Craig, in breaking this sad news to the Co-operators, referred to Thompson's announcement to him of his approaching demise. Such, he said, 'is the calmness with which philosophy can foresee and contemplate a change of existence.'

Extraordinary scenes were witnessed at the funeral of William Thompson in the churchyard of Dromberg near Glandore. Despite the dead man's atheist convictions, his nephew, one of the influential Whites of Bantry who expected to be his heir, insisted on his burial in consecrated ground according to Anglican rites. The parson, the Rev Jonas Travers Jones, reluctantly agreed in deference to a member of the leading gentry. In the graveyard, however, local hostility was actively manifested by both Catholics and Protestants. The leader of the demonstrators was a poor woman who clamoured against the interment of an 'infidel' besides her own God-fearing kindred. White of Bantry succeeded in silencing her with a sovereign, but she had barely traversed three fields when she stumbled in crossing a ditch and sprained her wrist, an accident she ascribed to Divine judgment. After the funeral followed the ceremony of reading Thompson's famous will, which was dated October 27, 1830. It was discovered to the general dismay that it forbade any priest, 'Christian, Mohammedan, or Hindu,' to meddle with his remains. When Parson Jones heard this he was enraged at having been induced to utter prayers 'over such a reprobate.'

In accordance with the will, Dr Donovan, a local medico, was obliged to exhume the body which had been bequeathed for public examination 'to aid in conquering the foolish and frequently most mischievous prejudice against the public examination of corpses.' The skeleton was to be transferred to the first Co-operative community established in Great Britain or Ireland. Donovan later asserted that the body had been bequeathed to him on condition of his 'stringing up the bones' and sending them 'as a memento of love' to Mrs Wheeler, to whom Thompson had been attached; there were most minute particulars as to the preparation of the skeleton and how the 'ribs were to be tipped with silver so that it might present a fashionable appearance.' What actually happened to Thompson's remains is uncertain, though Donovan states, and probably with truth, that Pierre Henri Baume, a Frenchman whom he terms a phrenologist, 'came across from London to claim the cranium to lecture on its physical development.'[1]

The most important feature of Thompson's will was, however, a quite different bequest. After laying aside an annuity of a hundred pounds for Anna Wheeler and a sum of £4,000 to be reserved to discharge any claims which might be advanced by the trustees of his father's estate, the residue of his property was bequeathed to the Co-operative Movement. Funds were to be lent to assist the establishment of communities, and to reprint the *Appeal, Labour Rewarded*, and the whole or such parts of the *Inquiry* as his trustees might 'deem most useful.' Shares in Co-operative communities were to be purchased and given to 'industrious persons, particularly young females' who could not otherwise afford to enter. Fifty pounds a year was to be devoted to Co-operative tours and lectures. All the deceased's books, maps, and engravings were to be presented to the first Co-operative community. By a codicil made on March 9, a fortnight before Thompson's death, John Jagoe of Bantry, County Cork, was appointed executor, and the trustees were to comprise Anna Wheeler, John Minter Morgan, John Finch, Henry MacCormac, John Scott Vandeleur, and a number of Irishmen mostly residents of County Cork.

The news of Thompson's death, writes Holyoake, came as 'a matter of deep regret to all social reformers.' The Radical *Working Man's Friend* 'deplored' the death of 'so truly patriotic a gentleman.' A memorial oration on the 'highly esteemed, enlightened and philanthropic' comrade was delivered at the Salford Co-operative Institution, the ceremony closing with a hymn by G. Mandley paraphrasing Pope's *Vital Spark*:

> Midnight gloom o'er spreads the day!
> One who shed a glorious ray
> On our hopes, is now departed;
> To that shore his soul's departed,
> Silent shore from out whose bourne
> Traveller never did return.
>
> Pity drooping hangs her head
> Sorrowing o'er our Thompson dead;
> Mourns Philanthropy a son
> Death – stern Death, has from her won.
> Tell, O Guardian Angels, tell,
> Was lost our cause when Thompson fell?
>
> Hark! Voices sweet salute our ears,
> Hope list'ning triumphs o'er our fears,
> For joyful news they bring,
> Millions of souls shall yet be free!
> Then Grave where is thy Victory?
> O Death, where is thy sting?

Thompson's followers were shocked by the loss of the leader upon whom they had relied to guide them to the promised land of communities. Nevertheless, they were inspired with new hope by his generous bequest, which had come at a time when they were beginning to lose hope of raising the necessary funds. Minter Morgan declared that Thompson's will 'deserved to be read in the market-place of every town in the Empire,' for 'he had given his days and nights to the furtherance of justice: As the welfare of the species was the subject of his continual meditation and of his unwearied efforts, so in his last moments he remembered the sacred cause to which his valuable life and great talents had been dedicated.'

The fifth Co-operative Congress adopted resolutions of gratitude for the 'important services' which their late 'much respected friend' had rendered and for his bequest which made 'even his death conduce to that end to which he had devoted his life.' Thanks were voted to Jagoe and Pare, both of whom had gone to Ireland to arrange the transfer of the property, and a committee was appointed to raise funds to meet what were regarded as purely legal formalities.

It soon became evident, however, that the Co-operators would not be allowed to inherit their legacy without considerable opposition, for Thompson's relatives had intervened to oppose the will. Owen hastened to Ireland in alarm. On returning to London he reported that the property was valuable, but that a contest must be expected. Baume, anxious to keep 'a watchful eye over the appropriation of the late Mr Thompson's property,' invited 'all practical men and women' to form a Co-operative Metropolitan Guardians' Committee. By August news reached London that although the trustees had been permitted to take conditional possession of the property, which was valued at between fifteen and sixteen thousand pounds, the order had been countermanded as soon as the relatives had lodged in the Irish Court of Chancery what the Co-operators regarded as an 'invalid claim.' To kill any idea that their lack of funds might prevent them from defending their interests, Jagoe wrote to his friends in Ireland urging them to impress on everyone they met that 'no means will be wanting to prosecute the suit.' Pare appealed in the *Crisis* and the *'Destructive' and Poor Man's Conservative* for funds, declaring that the relatives had offered a compromise, but that the Co-operators had consulted two eminent Irish barristers, who had advised that the property was legally vested in the trustees. As the case was to be heard in November one of the trustees had to proceed at once to Ireland to assist in the defence. Pare declared himself unable to go unless assistance were forthcoming, for the trustees had already advanced 'more than they could well afford.' This appeal evoked a prompt response, which enabled him to sail to Ireland, where he combined his activities in respect of the legal proceedings with commercial work for the Birmingham Co-operative Labour Exchange.

It would seem that tempers ran high in Ireland for Warden is found expressing thanks to Jagoe for the zeal and ability with 'which he had even risked his life' in defending the property 'against an outrageous attack by the opposing party.' By December, dissatisfaction among the London Co-operators burst into flame. At a meeting on December 11, Warden read Thompson's will to spur the audience to renewed effort, and Baume in a 'voice of contagious force and impassioned manner' moved a resolution of 'disgust and alarm' at 'the attempts being made by the party of idlers to deprive the industrious classes' of the bequest of the 'highly gifted philanthropist.' Thus stimulated, the meeting readily pledged its support for the 'arduous task' of the trustees by a collection of six pounds eighteen shillings – almost a pound more than had been amassed by the committee for community building upon which Thompson and Owen had clashed the year before. Warden, Anna Wheeler, and Mrs Grenfell were among the Co-operators appointed to raise funds 'by every means' to ensure the fulfilment of the will. They were to hold a Christmas Day Festival with refreshments, a concert, 'splendid entertainment' and dancing till one in the morning.

The lure of the estate stimulated Co-operators throughout the country. A Social Festival was held in the Salford Town Hall on Whit Monday of 1834; the National Equitable Exchange Association, the Norwich Co-operative Society, and other bodies were also active. By March sixty pounds had been raised. Pare reckoned that by raising as much again it would be possible to take out probate, regain possession of the property, and defend the will in a Chancery suit if necessary. A friend, mindful that Anna Wheeler was being kept waiting for her legacy, wrote to the *Crisis* enclosing five pounds and promising a similar amount each quarter 'until the trustees obtain justice.'

The processes of law were long and complicated. The Consistory Court of Dublin appointed a Commission which adopted the unusual course of proceeding to Cork to examine the will and hear witnesses; but the Proctor employed by the relatives declined to cross-examine the Co-operators. The Commissioners, fully satisfied with the authenticity of the documents and the evidence of the witnesses, reported to the Court in support of the will. The relatives countered by seeking to set it aside on the plea that the testator was insane, but declined to submit proof when the time to present it arrived. They now admitted the validity of the will, urging their claim not as Thompson's heirs but as his creditors and the heirs of his father, the late Alderman Thompson. They alleged that in 1807 the deceased, being in financial difficulties, had borrowed money from his father; though Thompson had provided £4,000 to meet any such claim, they succeeded in obtaining a conditional order in bankruptcy and the appointment of an official receiver. Taken by surprise, the Co-operators had not the time to contest this new strategem. Of the thirteen trustees, eight resident in Ireland had refused to act. Jagoe, Scott Vandeleur, Anna Wheeler, and three English Co-operators were left to defend the will.

On January 14, 1834, the bankruptcy order came up for confirmation

at the Roll's Court, Dublin. The trustees found themselves opposed by
Thompson's sisters, Miss Lydia Thompson and Mrs Sarah Dorman
and the husband of the latter, Thomas Dorman, who, in accordance
with the laws the Irish Socialist had assailed, had sole legal power to
act for his wife. The relatives now sought to impute insolvency to
Vandeleur, who had just gambled away his estate at Ralahine, and to
Jagoe, whom they alleged was living 'on board ship' to avoid the
bailiffs. Still more serious, they declared that the object of the will was
to foster Thompson's aims, which 'distinctly avowed an intention to
abolish marriage.' Despite the protests of the Co-operators' lawyers,
extracts from a copy of *Practical Directions* which the author had presented to his sisters, were read aloud in the solemn atmosphere of the
Court burdened with its ancient forms and customs. The audience,
steeped in convention, completely unschooled in the reasoning of advanced social philosophy, heard with horror and amazement a succession of excerpts from the deceased's most daring and unconventional
writings. They learned that marriage was 'irrevocable despotism' based
on the 'caprice and ascetism' of 'various editions of superstition' and
clothed in 'arbitrary and entirely unessential ceremonies.' Sexual
intercourse in the future would be governed by 'enlightened reason
with happiness solely in view,' arrangements being made to avoid
imprudent increase of numbers. The burden of childbearing would fall
'as a matter of course on those women whose organization was best
adapted to it – the healthiest, the finest formed, and those likely to
suffer the least inconvenience.' These ideas, declared the Counsel for
the relatives, sought 'to annul marriage altogether' and were 'contrary
to the laws of God and man.' A will which 'tended to promulgate and
perpetuate such immorality, ought not to be sanctioned by a Court of
Justice.'

The Master of the Rolls then gave judgment. He observed that
whilst the 'immorality and illegality' of part of the will might necessitate the estate being vested in the Crown, its nature was irrelevant to the
issue whether the relatives had any claim as creditors. On the other
hand, because the sum claimed by the relatives exceeded the value of
the estate, it was impossible to allot the trustees any portion of the
estate at that stage, and since the debtor was dead and a new succession
had occurred the trustees had little claim to the usufruct of the land.
Again, since so many of them had refused to act, the powers of all were
temporarily suspended until new trustees should be duly appointed.
Jagoe's insolvency, though not sufficient as an independent ground as

the plaintiffs declined to raise the matter, was yet a strong adjunct fact. Also the relatives had a claim as heirs, even although they had not in fact formally disputed the will on this ground, regarding it 'a waste of money to do so.' He therefore declared they had a *prima facie* claim to be considered as creditors, and made absolute the conditional order for a receiver in bankruptcy.[2]

Though the Master of the Rolls had thus dashed the immediate hopes of the Co-operators, the claim of the relatives had still by no means been proved. It was clear that to disprove what was considered an entirely bogus claim would be a lengthy affair.

The Co-operators, however, did not lose hope. They discussed the will at length at the First Congress of the Association of All Classes of All Nations, and again at the National Community Friendly Society, which met in Birmingham in 1839, six years after Thompson's death. Finch now declared that all the original thirteen trustees, save Pare, Jagoe, and himself, were dead or had resigned. The cost of the proceedings had amounted to well on three hundred pounds, but Jagoe feared 'he had done little or nothing in the affair.' Pare, however, was confident as usual; he declared that opposition had been instigated by an attorney 'who bore but an indifferent character' and had finally decamped to America, since when the relatives had taken no further steps and had apparently abandoned the case. Serjeant O'Loghlen, who had been leading Counsel for the Co-operators, had been appointed Master of the Rolls, and another of their legal advisers had become Attorney-General for Ireland. The Birmingham Co-operator naively regarded these as 'hopeful signs'; he urged that the Co-operative case should be drawn up by Dublin solicitors and laid before 'a good English lawyer.' An application should be made to the Court Receiver for funds to prosecute the case!

The much-desired estate was never secured by the Co-operators. The will was marooned in the Irish Court of Chancery for more than twenty-five years by the almost interminable processes of the law against which the deceased had inveighed. Year after year legal authorities and precedents were quoted. At last, when lawyers' fees and Court costs had devoured the greater part of the estate, judgment was given for the relatives on most counts. The precise terms of the decision are unknown, the records having been burnt along with the will itself in the conflagration of the Dublin Four Courts during the Sinn Fein rebellion of Easter 1916. When, however, Thompson's sisters won the case, the estate was so heavily mortgaged to meet the legal costs that it had to be sold by order of the Incumbered Estates Court. Holyoake alleges that Pare 'obtained some residue' from the estate which enabled him to issue an abbreviated version of the *Inquiry*, which was published with a preface by himself in 1850 and reissued with a new preface in 1869. Holyoake, who records that works of William Thompson were still in print in 1875, criticizes Pare's failure to disclose the sum received or to give 'any details of the expenditure of the trust funds.' His comment on the fate of the will is that 'it was impossible to leave money for purposes of social or mental progress, not of a conventional, orthodox character'; 'nobody believed in the sanity of anyone who sought unknown improvements in an untrodden way.'

18

Aftermath

The failure to obtain Thompson's estate symbolized the collapse of the community movement to which he had devoted his dying years. His importance in social history does not, however, rest upon his advocacy of communities. Schemes of community building might pass into oblivion, but the Co-operative Movement, of which he was one of the two foremost protagonists, directed a searching analysis to the economic system which led to a widespread demand for equality of distribution and the total erosion of the capitalist system. The Co-operators were active at the birth of British Socialism; they fashioned its basic doctrines and won its first converts. Their analyses, polemics, and Utopias fostered Socialist ideas and values among minds hitherto wholly unschooled in social affairs, and the spirit of revolt engendered by their propaganda produced many an unexpected harvest.

The importance of William Thompson's writings, and the influence of the school of thought to which he belonged, is to be seen in a number of distinct and widely separate fields, which must now be scanned, as they are essential to any appraisal of his work.[1]

Anti-property Economics

The Industrial Revolution compelled all whom it affected to ponder the problems it thrust upon them, but the rich and the poor started from different standpoints: the rich from the abstractions of property, the poor from the facts of their own lives. The 'political economy' of the *laissez-faire* economists, and the Socialist doctrine of exploitation, emerged as rival ideologies in a nation which, as Disraeli said, was really 'two nations.'

The growth of the doctrine of exploitation during Thompson's lifetime is an important facet of social history. Its rise transformed working-class politics and falsified the expectations of the Philosophic Radicals, who pinned their faith to Benthamite Utilitarianism and *laissez-faire* economics; for the anti-capitalist theories struck at the heart of the emerging capitalist system, providing both intellectual arguments and a battle cry for all who championed the rights of the labourers in the 'dark satanic mills' of early industrialism.

The doctrine won rapid acceptance among large sections of the British working class because it sprang naturally from the circumstances of their lives under the rigours of the new industrialism. It appealed to the British labourer in Thompson's day for the very same reason that gave it popularity in Europe when reformulated a generation or so later by Marx; as Laski explains, it was popular not by virtue of 'any logical estimation' of its 'theoretic adequacy,' but because to the worker it was 'the natural explanation' of his oppressed condition; it summarized 'the most poignant experience he knew.'[2]

In early nineteenth-century England the doctrine was expounded by the so-called Ricardian Socialist school, all of whom, while basing their economic theories on those of Ricardo, were champions of the rights of labour against the claims of capital. Foxwell, one of the main authorities on the school, considers Thompson its most important exponent on account of the completeness of his exposition, the wide influence of his writings, and his utter devotion to the cause. His thought, Foxwell adds, deserves 'the serious attention of all concerned with social philosophy,' being 'closely reasoned, original in conception, striking at the very root of the principles on which existing society was based, and expounded in such a vigorous fashion as to exert widespread influence over the mass of people at that time distressed and disaffected.'[3]

It is no exaggeration to assert that many early English Socialists, in their eager efforts to explain the cataclysm of emerging industrial Capitalism, regarded his *Inquiry* as a 'Bible of the Industrious Classes,' meticulously studying it almost as the Protestant reformers had devoted themselves to the Bible, and in much the same way as rebel spirits on the Continent were soon to turn to the writings of Marx and Engels. Thompson's writings were widely quoted in Co-operative publications and frequently discussed in working-class gatherings, and had served as 'texts' for Sunday 'services' at New Harmony and elsewhere. This enthusiastic veneration was voiced by Minter Morgan:

> Mr Thompson was one of those extraordinary minds which seem to start into existence at the very epoch they are most wanted – in times only of great difficulty and public distress, when the social edifice

seems tottering to its fall, and all the elements of the moral world wage war with existing institutions. It is at such a moment the enlightened philanthropist appears, and sets himself to the calm investigation of the hidden causes of human misery, poverty and crime; and so absorbed was Mr Thompson in this inquiry, that he may be said to have lost his own individuality in the pursuit: we find him identified with the whole of human kind. Like Pliny watching the combustion of Vesuvius, Mr Thompson's more useful investigation of moral phenomena in its threatened eruption continued to the last hour; and till Nature herself sounded his retreat, he ceased not his benevolent labours.'[4]

Thompson's influence was greatly extended by the support given to his ideas by such writers as Thomas Hodgskin, John Gray of Edinburgh, John Francis Bray of Leeds, and by the existence of the great Co-operative Movement. Foxwell lists over fifty newspapers disseminating Socialist ideas in the two decades 1820–40. Holyoake relates that during the Birmingham Co-operative Congress, at which Thompson played so important a role, over half a million leaflets were distributed. Owen sometimes spent as much as £4,000 in two months on propaganda; he would purchase up to 30,000 copies of a newspaper which had published one of his addresses, for instance for dispatch to the clergy, causing such a bulk of additional postage that on one occasion the mail coaches were delayed twenty minutes in starting from St Martin's-le-Grand. By the end of the eighteen-thirties the Co-operators were circulating tracts at the rate of 2,000,000 in three years, and the 'Co-operative missionaries' Thompson had instituted were regularly visiting 350 towns, giving as many as 1,450 lectures a year, 604 of them on theology and ethics. In Manchester 1,000 pamphlets were distributed every Sunday; 40,000 were annually given away in London; fifty pounds was raised at a single meeting from the sale of literature. Engels records that every Socialist institution and most trade unions and Chartist groups ran schools where 'a purely proletarian education' was given, 'free from the influences of the bourgeoisie,' and also libraries where 'proletarian journals and books' were to be found. Flora Tristan, after a visit to England in 1839, computed that, out of a population of sixteen millions, at least half a million were Socialist. 'Every hall in the kingdom that could be hired,' claims Holyoake, 'resounded with debate; the corner of every street had its group of disputants; every green and open place where speakers could hold forth was noisy with controversy.'[5]

Francis Place, who followed the orthodox economists in their rejection of the doctrine of exploitation, has nevertheless provided invaluable documentation on the spread of Thompson's ideas. He tells of 'revolutionary' concepts, first formulated in London, finding their way to the Working-class leaders in Lancashire and the North of England, and of wide sections of the poorer classes being 'misled and bewildered' by Socialist ideas. Leaflets advocating the labourer's right to the product of his toil were being sold at twelve a penny; 'I have thirteen of these handbills, each on a separate subject, and all teaching the same doctrine.' At the Southwark Rotunda and other London meeting-places the same ideas were advocated, he says, by 'remarkably ignorant, but fluent speakers, filled with bitter notions of animosity against everybody who did not concur in the absurd notions they entertained.' 'Most of these men,' Place asserts, were 'loud and long talkers, vehement, resolute, reckless rascals,' who entertained the 'strange notion,' that *they* were *the* working people.' 'In a few and only a few instances was he able to convince trade unionists of the absurdity of the notion that everything produced in manufactures belongs solely to the people who make it.' The 'great body of the working people' was 'open to the delusions of the ill-informed and dishonest agitators,' who founded their doctrines on 'inherent rights' and 'notions of equality in respect of property.' This 'infatuation' had come to be accepted in varying degrees by 'nearly all men who in any sense of the word could be designated politicians of the working class.' It had even been embraced by numerous 'tradesmen, manufacturers, gentlemen, clergymen and professional men' who co-operated with the workers and 'either led them or supported their schemes' with a zeal which would 'only be abandoned' after 'repeated false steps and their consequent disappointments' had taught them wisdom. Almost the entire unstamped Press was inculcating its readers with 'absurd and mischievous doctrines respecting the right to property.'[6]

James Mill expressed similar fears. In October 1831 he wrote in anxiety to Place about a 'deputation of the working classes' who had been preaching Communism to Black, the editor of the *Morning Chronicle*:

Their notions about property look ugly ... they seem to think that it should not exist, and that the existence of it is an evil to them.

Rascals, I have no doubt, are at work among them ... the thing needs looking into.

Place replied that the contamination was largely emanating from the meetings at the Rotunda in Blackfriars Road and the Philadelphian Chapel in Finsbury. He was alarmed that such doctrines should be infiltrating into the *Morning Chronicle*, and explained that it was happening through the medium of Hodgskin, one of Black's subeditors.

The elder Mill was not satisfied. He wrote to Brougham:

Nothing can be conceived more mischievous than the doctrines which have been preached to the common people. The illicit cheap publications, in which the doctrine of the right of the labouring people, who they say are the only producers, is very generally preached, are superseding the Sunday newspapers and every other channel through which the people might get better information.[7]

Mill complained that Black was 'not very sharp in detecting' these views, and failed sufficiently to understand they might produce a 'subversion of civilized society, worse than the overwhelming deluge of Huns and Tartars.'

To counter this apprehended peril the Society for the Diffusion of Useful Knowledge published a pamphlet, entitled *The Rights of Industry*, denouncing the 'mischievous ignorance' of the Socialists. Anti-property doctrines, the labourers were warned,

sometimes meet you in the violent addresses that wrong-headed men deliver in popular assemblies. Sometimes they force themselves upon your notice in the shape of miserable writings, which profess to advocate your interests against those who are called your oppressors – by which name all are meant who have anything to lose, and anything to defend. Sometimes they are proclaimed aloud from 'Rotundas' where the priest of Atheism and the orator of Plunder stand side by side. And lastly, they insinuate themselves to your view, scattered among sound principles, intended to explain to you the laws which govern the production of wealth, in lectures on 'Popular Political Economy.' One and all of these counsellors, we say, are your bitterest enemies.

Such doctrines, apparently 'harmless as abstract propositions,' would end in 'maddening passion, drunken frenzy, unappeasable tumult, plunder, fire and blood.' Workers should remember the proverb, 'when two men ride on one horse, one man must ride behind' and understand that capital and labour were destined in the same fashion 'to perform a journey together to the end of time.'[8] To persuade the workers of this 'unpleasant truth' Mrs Marcet and Miss Martineau published popular booklets on what they considered the morals of political economy, many of them in the form of short stories. Hodgskin's anti-capitalist lectures on economics at the London Mechanics' Institute were suspended, the chairman, the Duke of Sussex, having warned members against debating political or theological subjects. Education, Engels complained, had to be rendered 'tame, flabby and subservient' if the worker was to regard competition as a sacred idol and 'resign himself to starvation.'

The challenge of Thompson and his school was in the main received in silence by the orthodox economists. Every now and then, however, a stray member of the fold felt obliged to refer to the 'pernicious' and 'dangerous' views which continued to spread. Professor Longfield, at Trinity College, Dublin, bemoaned that anti-capitalist theories were liable to 'stimulate the passions of the poor and ignorant,' but announced that he would not answer them because he knew he could not convert their exponents, who he was 'persuaded' could 'never make any impression' upon his College.[9] Another economist, Samuel Read, who observed that the labourers had been 'flattered and persuaded that they produce all,' attempted to rebut the Socialist case by protesting that 'the labourers must be informed and made to understand, that they *do not* produce all.'[10] On the other side of the Atlantic the American economist, Thomas Cooper, declared his primary task was to destroy the 'modern notions of Political Economy' spread 'among the operatives or mechanics,' by Thompson and Hodgskin and by their American disciples, Langdon Byllesby, Al. Ming, and Thomas Skidmore. After having described the claims of the workers as formulated in terms of the labour theory of value, he enunciated this harsh Malthusian answer which the capitalist would return to the labourer:

How came you here? Either your parents fixed you here for their convenience, or you came here for your own. Did *I* bring you into existence? Did *I* contract to find you employment? Did not your existence here take place without my procuration or concurrence, without my knowledge? Am I to be deprived of my property, robbed and punished, because your parents were thoughtless? Receive employment on my terms, or use your skill and strength where you please elsewhere![11]

Trade Unionism

Thompson's doctrines were expounded to the trade unionists by the energetic William Pare, who had been appointed the first 'Co-operative missionary' and who proclaimed himself the disciple of 'the celebrated' William Thompson. He toured the provinces as a 'Co-operative missionary' and lectured to the Manchester Mechanics' Institute, the Manchester Dressers' and Dyers' Society, and similar bodies. He was also a frequent contributor to the *United Trades' Co-operative Journal*, a weekly organ of trade unionists and Co-operators in the North of England read by close on 30,000 workers, and a delegate to the National Association for the Protection of Labour, at which he played an active part along with Doherty and Henry Hetherington.

Pare expounded all his master's doctrines. He explained that Co-operators were not oblivious of the need either for political reform or for trade unionism, though they realized that exploitation could never be removed by these remedies alone. The National Association, Pare urged, should employ their funds in establishing productive enterprises as Thompson had suggested. Union funds could best be utilized in supplying work to the unemployed in trade disputes; they would thus check the exactions of capitalists and prove that capital could be accumulated without capitalists as Thompson had said. It was his 'fervent prayer' that Co-operators and advocates of trade unions would not quarrel with each other, but would march forward in unison.[12] Thompson's views also received sterling support from Dr William King, the Brighton Co-operator, as well as from William Carpenter, who reprinted extracts from the Irish Socialist's writings on trade unionism in pamphlet form.[13]

The influence of Co-operative ideas on the trade-union movement was on any showing considerable. The very names of trade-union journals, *The United Trades' Co-operative Journal*, *The Union Pilot and Co-operative Intelligencer*, *The Voice of the People*, and the *Herald of the Rights of Industry*, reflect the ideas of Thompson and his group. It is significant, too, that Owen's famous Grand National Consolidated Trades Union was instituted at a joint conference of Co-operative and

Trade Societies held in the Co-operative Institution in London; as G. D. H. Cole observes, it was the Co-operators' sixth national Congress, and the successor to the Huddersfield Congress at which Thompson's death was announced.[14] The resolutions passed by the 'Grand National' are fully in the Thompson tradition, advocating that the 'productive classes' should free themselves from 'subservience to the money capitalists' by securing land upon which to labour for themselves. Their object, as the *Poor Man's Guardian* explained, was 'to establish for the productive classes a complete dominion over the fruits of their own industry.'

By the early eighteen-forties Engels remarked that the Socialists, though still 'a very small fraction' of the total British working class, were, nevertheless, 'its most educated and solid elements.'[15] Despite their pacifism and the opposition of Owen and others (not including Thompson) to political action, Laski considered that their advocacy of the right to the whole produce of labour contributed largely towards making this period one of 'revolutionary fervour.'[16] The Webbs observed that trade unions were emboldened to adopt 'haughty and contemptuous language' towards their employers, and that this was nothing more than an expression of the trade unionists' feeling that they were the only producers of wealth and hence the rightful directors of industry.[17]

Chartism

The great Chartist Movement owed its origin to William Lovett and a group of London Co-operators who drew inspiration from Thompson's *Labour Rewarded*, which had argued that friends of Co-operation could not 'reason consequently if they are not friendly to equal political institutions.' Rejecting Owen's proscriptions of political action, they had taken advantage of his visit to America in 1828–29 to launch a movement which sought, as Place avers, 'to blend their own peculiar views of society, especially on the production and distribution of wealth, with those of the Radical Reformers.'[18] They had 'read and admired the writings of Robert Owen, Thompson, Morgan and Gray, and had resolved to be instrumental to the extent of their means and abilities in spreading a knowledge of these works, throughout the country.' To this end they had founded the British Association for the Spread of Co-operative Knowledge, which held meetings at the London Rotunda, where their espousal of the burning issues of the day endeared them to a wide section of the London working class, thereby alarming Place and the elder Mill.

According to William Carpenter the Association changed its name to the National Union of the Working Classes in May 1831, in response to the Manchester meeting of the National Union for the Protection of Labour which had passed resolutions making the typically Thompsonian claim that, as workers, they maintained the nobility, the clergy, the merchants, the manufacturers, the shopkeepers, the publicans, the soldiers, and 'the menials of all these and the very dogs and horses of those who affect to despise us.' The change in name was not accompanied by any immediate change in ideology or tactics. The 'Aims and Objects' of the newly styled National Union wrote of its intention to secure 'for every working man the full value of his labour and the free disposal of his labour' and 'to protect working men against the tyranny of masters and manufacturers by all just means as circumstances may determine.'

Even after the formal change of name, the organization also continued to operate under its old title. As the Co-operative body it gave sterling support to Thompson's community plans and supported him in his struggle with Owen, while as the Union it held a meeting in Copenhagen Fields to commemorate the anniversary of the Second French Revolution, an essential political manifestation. The speakers were Hibbert, Warden, Cleave, Lovett, and Watson, all of whom were also active supporters of Thompson's attempt to establish a community.

The 'Union' remained under Co-operative influence. Two of its council members, Detrosier and Saul, were leading advocates of Co-operation; its library contained copies of Thompson's *Inquiry*; its manifestos declared labour 'the source of wealth,' and argued that 'until the labourers acquire sufficient knowledge to co-operate together, turn the power of machinery to their own account, and retain the produce of their own labour, they will remain poor in the midst of plenty, and ever be slaves in the land of freedom.' It claimed that Co-operation was 'beginning to be appreciated by thousands and tens of thousands of workmen,' but that a boycott of politics was impracticable; 'the government had declared war' upon the people, and it was necessary to be 'prepared to meet it.' Legislative action would, moreover, be needed to gain the people's rights.

The Chartist Movement remained largely in the hands of Co-operators and former Co-operators. The *English Chartist Circular*, which was founded by a group of Thompson's old comrades in 1841, bears a Socialist imprint which is unmistakable, and contains extracts from the writings of 'the philanthropic Mr Thompson'; though primarily concerned with the advocacy of Chartism, it carried articles highly sympathetic to Co-operation, which it termed 'the tendency of the times.' It held that Chartists should initiate Co-operative stores; they should 'rest assured' that nothing was 'better calculated ultimately to secure the Charter' than the destruction of the 'rampant power of the master class of millocrats and shopocrats'; social happiness could not be perfected unless the law-making power were in the hands of the people, but before perfect freedom could be enjoyed the social system itself would have to be remodelled.

Many of the Chartist leaders, among them Lovett, Bronterre O'Brien, Henry Hetherington, William Benbow, James Watson, and William Carpenter, served their apprenticeship under Thompson in the Co-operative Movement, and carried their Socialist ideas into the Chartist Movement, where a not insignificant leaven of the rank and file were Co-operators.[19] Engels asserted in 1845 that 'nearly all' the Chartist leaders were Socialists or Communists, while Samuel Kydd, writing in 1852, declared that many ardent Radicals and Chartists had been members of Co-operative stores for more than twenty years. That it was easy for Co-operators to be good Chartists is evident from Thompson's writings, which are sympathetic to all the ideas later embodied in the Charter. His great friend and disciple, William Pare, was one of the thirty-six founding members of the Birmingham Political Union, a body concerned primarily with the winning of a democratic franchise.

Latter-day Co-operation

Even if the Co-operative Movement in the decades which followed Thompson's death was devoted almost wholly to retail trading, it was to a significant degree the heir of the earlier movement. Many of the early Co-operators and their converts lived on, and deep down many of their original ideas survived.

In the annals of latter-day Co-operative history many of the old names and not a few of the old ideas recur again and again with surprising frequency. John Finch, who had played a prominent part at the Congresses of 1830 and 1831, who had visited Thompson at Glandore and was one of the trustees of his will, became the Governor of the

Queenswood Community, and was elected chairman of the Co-operative Congress of 1843. Benjamin Warder, another important figure at
the Congresses in Thompson's time, and one of the founders of the
National Union of the Working Classes, became president of the East
London Hall of Science.

In 1869 Thompson's most faithful disciple, William Pare, following
the old tradition, took the initiative in convening the Co-operative
Congress of that year, and was elected the first general secretary of the
Co-operative Central Board. He declared that 'after a quarter of a
century of shopkeeping it was surely time' to assume 'a higher platform
and a nobler task.' Paraphrasing the thought of his old master, he
urged the need to free the workers from the uncertainties of bad trade
and 'money panics'; land should be leased with power to purchase;
'self-supporting industrial colleges or villages' should then be erected
so that Co-operators could 'raise the necessaries of life' and be 'for ever
placed not only above the fear of want but in possession of all the
comforts of life.'

Joseph Styles and George Wigg also addressed the Congress as they
had done over three decades earlier when Thompson was still among
them. Dixon, looking back across the years to those first Congresses,
mused that he had 'begun very early,' while Campbell, another 'vet-
eran of the good cause' and now a leading force in Scottish trade
unionism, sent a message that he would report the Congress in the
Glasgow Sentinel.

In the columns of Pitman's *Co-operator* of the eighteen-sixties there
are other links with the past. The second reprint of Thompson's *Inquiry*
is advertised; there are letters from his old friends, Matthew Davenport
Hill, the Recorder of Birmingham, and Dr King of Brighton. Lectures
by E. T. Craig of Ralahine, to whom the Irish Socialist had presented a
copy of his *Practical Directions* during his visit to that Co-operative, are
announced. Craig had by this time introduced to the Co-operative
Movement John Green, who in his turn had converted Lloyd Jones,
one of the future historians of the working class. Abel Haywood, who
after Thompson's death had bought up the 'remainders' of his published works, was now an Alderman of the Manchester City Council,
but retained his Co-operative associations. Another old comrade,
Joseph Smith, who had taken part in the early Congresses and had
subsequently been active in the Queenswood Community, returned
from America after thirty years' absence 'unchanged in appearance, in
voice or fervour.' In his old age he became editor of the *Co-operative*

News, and wrote that within the English Co-operative Movement he was still 'doing fierce battle for Communism.'

The Co-operator was deeply imbued with the traditions of the early pioneers. One of its correspondents remarked that, however great might have been the failure of the early projects, it must not be supposed that they had left no permanent effect. In nearly every large town in the kingdom there had emerged active spirits who, though 'flung to the ground amid the ruins of the social edifice' they had hoped to raise, had 'gathered themselves up again' and set to work on 'less ambitious but more practical projects.'

The many Co-operators who turned from abortive community building to successful Co-operative trading indicate that latter-day Co-operation was to a vital extent the outcome of the propaganda and theorizing of the pioneers. Pare himself was fully aware of this; commenting on an article by a certain Robert Stephens entitled 'The Unity of Capital and Labour,' which appeared in *The Co-operator* a few weeks before, he wrote:

I believe I can claim Robert Stephens as one of my numerous Co-operative grandchildren. I am informed that he was a pupil in the school attached to the Salford Social Institution, which was founded through the instrumentality of two men well known to many of the old Socialists still living, Joseph Smith and Joseph Rigby, who in their day laboured without ceasing in the great cause. These two worthies attended my lectures in the Mechanics' Institution, Manchester, and joined in the discussion which I always endeavoured to elicit on these occasions – taking the competitive side. I succeeded, however, in making them converts; and now after the lapse of nearly forty years, I am able to see some of its specific results; for Robert Stephens acquired his Co-operative Knowledge in consequence of his attending the meetings of the Salford Social Institution.

One has only to remind oneself that Pare was himself the disciple of Thompson and that his lectures in Manchester had the Irishman's *Labour Rewarded* for its text to trace the continuity of Co-operative thought through almost a century!

Pare was never oblivious of this fact. In his preface to the 1869 reprint of Thompson's *Inquiry* he pays homage to the Irish Socialist and relates that, under the influence of Thompson's ideas, he had induced his native town, Birmingham, to take the 'bold and decided step' of abolishing church rates in 1832 – thirty-six years before the rest of the country. The people of Birmingham had 'consistently and steadily' refused to pay them, despite 'several conflicts' which had involved him in 'the loss of much time and money and the risk of personal liberty itself.' Meanwhile, reforms had been achieved all over the world. Serfdom had ceased in Russia; slavery had been relaxed in the Ottoman Empire; Free Trade had been greatly extended; the advantages of free secular education had come to be accepted by a much wider section of the community. 'Perhaps the greatest advance of all' had been the establishment of the 'Lord St Leonards' Act,' by which the workers had won the right to have their claims submitted to arbitration; this had been a substantial gain, though the workers' position could never be satisfactory under the capitalist system.

19

Influence on John Stuart Mill

Thompson's attacks on the classical economists are significant as the prelude to a widespread later reaction against 'Manchesterism.' They are important especially for their influence on John Stuart Mill, an influence which was first observed by Foxwell and mentioned by H. L. Beales, though ignored by most other commentators.[1]

Foxwell's case is that 'up to Thompson's time political economy had been rather commercial than industrial' and that he was 'the first writer to elevate the question of a just distribution of wealth' to a position of supreme importance. Mill, who had followed him, had 'definitely subordinated' production to distribution, which was 'the great and distinguishing theme of his work.' Foxwell could not doubt 'that this change was largely due to Thompson,' whose influence on Mill was, he declared, 'conspicuous in more directions than one' and extremely important, as 'after the appearance of Mill's *Principles*, English economists for a whole generation were men of one book.'

Mill himself makes no acknowledgement of being influenced by Thompson, though there is ample evidence that he was familiar with his ideas. As a young man he had debated with him in the Chancery lane debates of 1825. How great was the influence of those debates on the young Mill in his formative years perhaps Mill himself did not fully realize. He never terminated his association with the Co-operators, of whom Thompson, as we know, was the foremost theoretician.[2] In his *Autobiography*, he refers to Thompson as 'a very estimable man with whom I was well acquainted,' and mentions both Thompson's *Inquiry* and the *Appeal* which had been prompted by the claim of the elder Mill that the interests of women were 'included' in those of their husbands and male relatives.

Up to Mill's time, as he himself observed, 'the institution of property had only by a few speculative writers been brought into question.' Thompson had been one of the first of those speculative writers. In the conclusion to his *Inquiry* he argued that 'Of all the sources of error in

150

reasonings respecting wealth, none have been more frequent, or more avoidable, than assuming that the circumstances surrounding the writer, in whatever country writing, were unavoidable and necessarily permanent.' 'Permanent or universal truths' could not be established 'on such partial and treacherous foundations.' A writer,

> surrounded all his life with certain moral features, accustomed to witness certain restraints and certain peculiarities of distribution, is apt to regard them as equally stationary as the natural features of the scenery around him. In admiration of the natural scenery, however wild, useless, or pernicious to his well-being, he is trained from infancy to bow down. In admiration of the existing institutions and their consequences he is trained to bow down in equal admiration, because they were created by human power, guided, as he is told, sometimes by human, sometimes by superhuman, wisdom. Whatever is, he is taught to reverence.[3]

The most significant characteristic of John Stuart Mill was that he learnt this lesson and was the first economist recognized as such in bourgeois circles to make a study of the alternatives to competitive capitalism. He followed Thompson in insisting that the laws of distribution were merely human institutions, that once things had been produced society could 'do with them what it likes' and 'place them at the disposal of whomsoever it pleases and on whatever terms.'[4] As he observes in his *Autobiography*, the 'general tone' which distinguished his *Principles* from those of his predecessors 'consisted chiefly in making the proper distinction between the laws of the Production of Wealth, which are real laws of nature dependent on the properties of objects, and the modes of its Distribution which, subject to certain conditions, depend on human will.'

His criticism of 'the common run of political economists' is reminiscent of Thompson. He protests that they deem the principles of distribution to be 'economic laws incapable of being defeated or modified by human effort, ascribing the same necessity to things dependent on the unchangeable conditions of our earthly existence and to those which, being but the necessary consequences of particular social arrangements, are merely co-extensive with these.'

John Stuart Mill was favourably predisposed to Co-operative ideas, and repeats many of Thompson's favourite arguments. To those who held that Communism would allow everyone to evade a fair share of work, he replied, as had Thompson, that 'the same difficulty exists under the system on which nine-tenths of the business of society is conducted: from the Irish reaper or hodman to the Chief Justice or the Minister of State, nearly all the work of society is remunerated by day wages or fixed salaries.' A factory operative had less personal interest in his work than a member of a Communist association, since unlike the latter he was not working for a partnership of which he was himself a member. Under Communism the master's eye would be replaced by 'the eye not of one master but of the whole community.' In the extreme case of 'obstinate perseverance in not performing the due share of work' the community would have the same resources which society now had for compelling conformity to the necessary conditions of the association, namely the right of expulsion. Like Thompson, he considered that though equality could receive acquiescence, a system whereby a handful of human beings weighed everybody in the balance, giving more to one and less to another, 'would not be borne unless from persons believed to be more than men, and backed by supernatural terrors.' To the Malthusian argument that Communism would destroy all restraint on the multiplication of mankind, he replied, as had Thompson, that 'Communism is precisely the state of things in which opinion might be expected to declare itself with greatest intensity against this kind of selfish intemperance.' As soon as excessive reproduction was seen as an 'unmistakable inconvenience' public opinion would reprobate, and if reprobation did not suffice, repress this or any other culpable self-indulgence.

We may conclude that Mill's long contact with Thompson and the early English Co-operators undoubtedly had a significant influence on him; it forced him out of the groove of classical economics, opened his mind to the vital importance of the distribution of wealth and the possibility of reforming it, and caused him to consider the practicability and advantages of a Socialist organization of society, thereby predisposing him to associate with Saint-Simonian and other later brands of Socialism.

20

Thompson and Marx: 'Scientific Socialism'

Thompson's political thought resembles in numerous respects the theoretical system of Karl Marx. Since any connection with so supremely controversial a thinker as Marx inevitably arouses heated debate both in academic and political circles, it is not surprising that many commentators have considered the works of Thompson with at least one eye turned on the author of the *Communist Manifesto* and *Capital*.

Anton Menger, who virtually re-discovered the 'right to the whole product of labour' group of Socialists, declares Thompson 'the most eminent founder of scientific socialism'[1] from whom 'the later Socialists, the Saint-Simonians, Proudhon, and above all, Marx and Rodbertus, have directly or indirectly drawn their opinions.' Thompson had taken 'his stand on a very advanced Socialism,' in which all Socialist philosophy of the right to the whole product of labour was 'completely expounded'; from his writings one could 'recognize at once' the 'train of thought, and even the mode of expression which reappear later on in the works of so many other Socialists, especially Marx and Rodbertus.' Marx was:

> Completely under the influence of the earlier English Socialists, and more particularly of William Thompson. Leaving out of account the mathematical formulae by which Marx rather obscures than elucidates his argument, the whole theory of surplus value, its conception, its name, and the estimates of its amount, are borrowed in all essentials from Thompson's writings. Only Marx, in accordance with the aim of his work, pays special attention to one form of unearned income (interest on capital), and fails to give either that jural criticism of private property in instruments of production and useful commodities which is the necessary supplement of the theory of surplus value, or a rigorous exposition of the rights to the whole product of labour. In all these respects Marx is far inferior to

153

Thompson, so that the work of the latter may be regarded as the foundation stone of Socialism.[2]

These claims have been widely accepted. Foxwell observes that though the early English Socialists were ignored for half a century 'by the official representatives of social philosophy in the country of their birth,' they were not dead because they 'remained germinating in the minds of Marx and Engels'; Laski declares that Thompson and his comrades were 'the men who laid the foundations' which Marx and Engels 'brought so remarkably to completion.'[3] Sidney and Beatrice Webb describe Marx as the 'illustrious disciple' of Thompson and Hodgskin;[4] Beales says that though Thompson's work did 'not lead to any visible millennium, it did lead to Marx';[5] Cole, on slightly different grounds, refers to Marxian Socialism as 'the weaving together of the writings of Hodgskin and Thompson's critique of the classical economists.'[6] Marshall opines that both Marx and Rodbertus borrowed from Thompson 'their practical conclusions as to the nationalization of the means of production and their theoretical arguments.'[7] Schumpeter elaborates the argument, observing that,

> the Socialist thinkers of the nonage provided many a brick and many a tool that proved useful later on. After all, the very idea of a Socialist society was their creation, and it was owing to their efforts that Marx and his contemporaries were able to discuss it as a thing familiar to everyone. Many of the Utopians went much farther. They worked out details of the Socialist plan, thereby formulating problems – however inadequately – and clearing much ground. Even their contribution to purely economic analysis cannot be neglected. It provided a much needed leaven in an otherwise stodgy pudding and stood Marx in good stead.[8]

Though the letter of the Foxwell-Menger thesis has been widely accepted, its spirit has not passed unchallenged. Simkhovitch, one of the most resolute critics of Marx, declares that, though 'not a single separate idea' was originated by him, it is 'folly to search for a predecessor from whom Marx borrows his system as the combination of these ideas in one colossal structure is Marx's own achievement.'[9] Veblen, another critic of Marx, has also emphasized that 'there is no system of economic thought more logical than that of Marx. No member of the system, no single article of doctrine, is fairly to be understood, criticized, or defended, except as an articulate member of the whole.' 'The Marxian theory of surplus value and exploitation,' is, therefore, 'not simply the doctrine of William Thompson, transcribed and sophisticated in a forbidding terminology, however great the superficial resemblance, and however large Marx's unacknowledged debt to Thompson may be on these heads.' Marx's system 'taken as a whole, lies within the frontiers of neo-Hegelianism; even the details are worked out in accordance with the preconceptions of that school of thought, and have taken on the complexion that would properly belong to them on that ground.'[10] Beer, again, has argued that what really distinguished Marx from Thompson was that he integrated the theory of exploitation with a Hegelian insight of the economic evolutionary process which 'made Utopia a science.'[11]

We do not know when 'the founder of scientific Socialism' first made the acquaintance of Thompson and his group. While still in Germany, Marx became a member of the 'Doctors' Club,' which was a 'mish-mash' of Chartist, Owenite, and Saint-Simonian ideas; and, later, he received news of the English movement from Engels, who settled here in 1842. The latter had early made the acquaintance of Robert Owen and James Watson, had attended Co-operative meetings in Manchester and had written for the *New Moral World*. In his *Condition of the Working Class in England in 1844* he does not mention Thompson and his group by name, though he is clearly alluding to them when he refers to a group of English Socialists who had 'succeeded in developing' the theories of Bentham and Godwin 'a step forward.' These writings, he declared, were 'far in advance of the whole bourgeois literature of intrinsic worth'; they were 'more ample' than their counterpart in France and had 'done wonders for the education of the proletariat.'[12] Elaborating this theme in later years, Engels declares that the conclusions of the Ricardian Socialists, which had been deduced 'with so much clearness and profundity,' had 'in great part' been rediscovered by Marx and 'could not be surpassed' until the appearance of *Capital* in 1867.[13]

Engels probably drew Marx's attention to this valuable literature, for he declares that he sent his friend copies or extracts of all the Socialist works which could be procured in Manchester.[14] We find in consequence that Marx first mentions Thompson in his *Poverty of Philosophy*, which he wrote in Paris in 1847, before he made his home in England. He remarks that 'nearly all' the English Socialists had 'proposed the egalitarian application of the Ricardian theory.'[15] He later refers to Thompson in his *Critique of Political Economy* of 1859, and in the first volume of *Capital* which appeared in 1867. These references, though they do little to indicate the extent of any debt to Thompson, nevertheless establish that Marx was acquainted with his work and had made a careful study of the *Inquiry*, the first reprint of which appeared the year after he settled in London.

Marx and Engels do not examine Thompson or any of the other Socialists of his time in detail. They are content to bracket them together under the title 'Utopian Socialists,' or to classify them into the schools of Owen, Saint-Simon, and Fourier. The *Communist Manifesto* is on the whole critical of its forebears, though it admits that they gave expression to the workers' 'first instinctive aspirations towards a thorough-going transformation of society,' and were 'of great value in promoting the enlightenment of the workers,' particularly in regard to the need for the 'obliteration of the contrast between town and country,' the 'transformation of the State into a mere instrument for the superintendence of production' and the 'abolition of the family, private gain and wage labour.'

Since the 'founders of scientific Socialism' make no attempt to assess the influence of Thompson's writings on their thought, the question, like that of the relationship between Thompson and Mill, must be left to internal evidence.

The Marxist analysis, which was developed a couple of decades later than that of Thompson, is, of course, vaster, subtler, and more detailed. It is more a text-book of economics, less a moral cry of protest. Seeking to be scientific if not academic, it often adopts mathematical exposition. It benefits from the fact that there then existed a more refined science of 'political economy' than prevailed at the time of its forerunner; moreover, its author was able to observe a more advanced stage of capitalism, which caused him to emphasize more heavily the role of exploitation in industrial as opposed to agricultural society.

Nevertheless, when all this is said, a remarkable similarity remains. Both writers adopt the labour theory of value and postulate that labour is the sole source of wealth. Both consider exploitation the fundamental of Capitalism, and believe that the basic function of economics should be to analyse the distribution of wealth between the productive and exploiting classes. Both attack the exactions of the 'unproductive' classes, but consider 'the right to the whole product of labour' Utopian and impossible to achieve within the capitalist system; both look forward to a classless Communist society in which private property is abolished and distribution accords with the precept 'to each according to his need, from each according to his ability.' Marx's famous theory of the 'withering away' of the State is also held by Thompson, who considers that in a Communist society 'almost all the occasions for the exercise of the ordinary functions of government would have ceased.'

The greatest similarity, however, occurs in the discussions on 'surplus value' – a term which both writers employ. Thompson's theory, like that of Marx, describes how exploitation arises out of the excessive bargaining strength of capitalists and landlords who can reduce the worker to absolute starvation if he rejects the terms they offer; Thompson, like 'the founder of scientific Socialism,' argues that the exploiting classes use the State machine to make class legislation for their own benefit. His definition of the State as 'the aristocratic law-making committee of the Idle Classes' is an interesting anticipation of its description in the *Communist Manifesto* as 'nothing more than a committee for the administration of the consolidated affairs of the bourgeois class as a whole.'[16] Similarly, his argument that public opinion in the past was nothing other than 'the opinion of the influential classes of society' is reminiscent of the declaration of Marx and Engels that 'the ruling ideas of each age have ever been the ideas of its ruling class.'[17]

Thompson considers the worker to be 'at the mercy' of the capitalists 'for whatever portion of the fruits of his own labour they may think proper to leave to his disposal in compensation for his toil.'[18] 'By far the greater part of the products of his labour' are taken from him by:

> those who have no further share in production than the accumulation and lending of such articles to the real operative producer. The idle possessor of these inanimate instruments of production procures ten times, a hundred times, a thousand times, as much of the articles of wealth as the utmost labour of such efficient producers can procure for them.

The productive labourers, 'stript of all capital, of tools, houses and materials to make their labour productive, toil from want, from the necessity of existence, their remuneration being kept at the lowest compatible with the existence of industrious habits'[19] [*sic*]. Twenty-four years later the authors of the *Communist Manifesto* wrote in similar vein, declaring that the worker is allowed no more than a wage which will 'support his bare existence and reproduce his kind.'

Thompson also foreshadows Marx in that he considers individuals are actuated by class interests, and that 'no high-sounding moral maxims influence or can influence the rich as a body,' for 'like all other classes in every community,' they must 'obey the influence of the peculiar circumstances in which they are placed.'[20] Marx and Engels concluded that the Capitalist system must inevitably bring about its own annihilation by engendering a class antagonism destined to destroy it; the old society, they argued, contained the new society in its womb, for the proletariat, the only 'really revolutionary' class, was 'always increasing in numbers' and becoming 'disciplined, united, organized by the very mechanism of the process of capitalist production itself.'[21] This idea is not so clearly expressed by Thompson, though he says: 'The Industrious Classes are now learning their own importance; they will soon speak out; and thenceforward, they alone will regulate human affairs, essentially their own affairs. The idle will lose the support of public opinion, and as a class will cease to exist.'[22]

Notes and References

Chapter 1

1. *Laski-Holmes Letters* (edited by Mark De Wolfe Howe) (1953), Vol. I, pp. 201, 205, 358.
2. J William Thompson, *Labour Rewarded* (1827), p. 1.

Chapter 2

1. *Bentham Papers*, 1818, p. 176.
2. *The Works of Jeremy Bentham* (edited by John Bowring), Vol. X, pp. 506–7.
3. *The Works of Jeremy Bentham*, Vol. X, p. 507.
4. *The Works of David Ricardo* (edited by Piero Sraffa).
5. British Museum Additional MSS. No. 33, 563.
6. Louisa Devey, *Life of Rosina, Lady Lytton* (1887), pp. 35–7.
7. William Thompson, *An Inquiry into the Principles of the Distribution of Wealth* (1824), p. x.
8. William Thompson, *Labour Rewarded*, pp. 98–9, 164; *An Inquiry into the Principles of the Distribution of Wealth*, p. 443.
9. Sidney and Beatrice Webb, *The History of Trade Unionism* (1920), pp. 162–3.

Chapter 3

1. The book will subsequently be referred to by this or other shortened forms.
2. *An Inquiry into the Principles of the Distribution of Wealth*, pp. xviii-xix.
3. ibid. p. 375.
4. ibid. pp. xv-xvi.
5. *An Inquiry into the Principles of the Distribution of Wealth*, pp. xiii-xiv.
6. ibid. p. 1.
7. *An Inquiry*, p. 21.
8. W. Stark, *The Ideal Foundations of Economic Thought* (1943), p. 103.
9. *Inquiry*, pp. 151–2.
10. ibid. p. 146.

11. British Museum Additional MSS. No. 27,952, folio 155; *Phosphor*, Vol. 1, No. 1, June 8, 1825, p. 4; *Macdonald Diaries*, pp. 165–6, 211.
12. John Minter Morgan, *The Revolt of the Bees* (1826), pp. 18, 81; *idem*, *Hampden in the Nineteenth Century* (1834), Vol. II, p. 301; *idem*, *The Reproof of Brutus* (1830), pp. 69–70.
13. *Indiana as Seen by Early Travellers* (edited by Harlow Lindley), pp. 387–8.
14. British Museum Additional MSS. No. 37,773, pp. 27–9.
15. W. Longson, *An Appeal to Masters, Workmen and the Public* (1827), pp. 15–32.
16. Jules Lechevalier, *Etudes sur la Science Sociale* (1834), p. 435.

Chapter 4

1. *An Inquiry into the Principles of the Distribution of Wealth*, pp. iii-vi.
2. *Inquiry*, pp. 19–27.
3. *Inquiry*, p. 73.
4. ibid. pp. 151–60.
5. *Inquiry*, pp. 88, 143–4, 157.
6. ibid. pp. 34–6, 88.
7. *Inquiry*, pp. 35, 40, 44.
8. *Inquiry*, pp. 44, 94–5, 257.
9. ibid. pp. 48, 81.
10. *Inquiry*, pp. 94, 583, 585.
11. *idem*, *Labour Rewarded*, pp. 10–12.
12. ibid. p. 95.
13. *Inquiry*, p. 97.
14. *Inquiry*, p. 40.
15. ibid. pp. 60, 65, 70, 169.
16. *Inquiry*, pp. 150, 164–5, 173, 270, 303, 586–9, 598–9.

Chapter 5

1. *Inquiry*, pp. 9–17.
2. *Inquiry*, p. 166.
3. *idem*, *Labour Rewarded*, p. 114.
4. *Inquiry*, p. 90.
5. ibid. pp. 11–13.
6. *Inquiry*, p. 167.
7. *Inquiry*, pp. 78, 165, 171.
8. ibid. pp. 171–2, 423.
9. These arguments, which were original in Thompson's day, were taken up a decade or so later by Sismondi, and many generations later found a place in the writings of K. Wicksell, J. A. Hobson, and V. I. Lenin.

10. *Inquiry*, pp. 164, 38–9.
11. *Inquiry*, pp. 39–40.
12. ibid. p. 164.
13. *Inquiry*, pp. 170–1.
14. ibid. pp. 218–19.
15. ibid. p. 422.
16. ibid. pp. 133, 220–1.
17. *Inquiry*, pp. 176, 423, 590, 594.

Chapter 6

1. *Inquiry*, pp. 516–18, 192–4.
2. ibid. pp. 369–74.
3. ibid. pp. 214–18.
4. *Inquiry*, pp. 183–4, 189–201.
5. *Inquiry*, pp. 189, 190, 195–9, 211–12, 217–21.
6. ibid. p. 259.
7. *Inquiry*, pp. 197–9, 220–2, 253, 370, 507.
8. ibid. pp. 190, 369, 378, 408.
9. *idem, Practical Directions* (1830), pp. 199–200.
10. *Inquiry*, pp. 379–80.

Chapter 7

1. T. R. Malthus, *An Essay on the Principles of Population* (1803), p. 531.
2. *Inquiry*, p. 535.
3. *Inquiry*, pp. 243, 426; *idem, Practical Directions*, pp. 229–30.
4. *Inquiry*, p. 426.
5. *Inquiry*, p. 426.
6. *Practical Directions*, pp. 231–2, 246.
7. *Inquiry*, pp. 536–7, 547–50.
8. ibid. pp. 556–7.
9. *Practical Directions*, p. 232.
10. ibid. p. 231.

Chapter 8

1. Erna Reiss, *Rights and Duties of Englishwomen* (1934), *passim*; Caroline H. Dall, *Woman's Rights under the Law* (1861), *passim*.
2. J. A. Perkins, *Life of Mrs Norton* (1909), *passim*; W. Lyon Blease, *The Emancipation of English Women* (1910), *passim*.
3. *Inquiry*, pp. 314–15.
4. *Practical Directions*, pp. 244–7.

5. Michael Sadleir, *Bulwer Lytton and his Wife* (1933), *passim*; Louisa Devey, *Life of Rosina, Lady Lytton* (1887) *passim*.

6. *Robert Owen Letters*, No. 426.

7. Richard K. P. Pankhurst, 'Saint-Simonism in England' in the *Twentieth Century Review*, December 1952 and January 1953.

8. William Thompson, *Appeal of One Half the Human Race, Women, against the Pretensions of the Other Half, Men, to restrain them in Political and thence in Civil and Domestic Slavery* (1825).

9. *Practical Directions*, pp. 244–7.

Chapter 9

1. *Appeal*, pp. 54–5.

2. The first Divorce Act was passed in 1858.

3. *Appeal*, p. 56.

4. It was not until the Jackson case of 1891, called 'the married woman's charter of personal liberty,' that the husband lost the legal right to imprison his wife in order to compel her to satisfy his conjugal rights.

5. *Appeal*, pp. 70, 78–9, 85.

6. In Thompson's day a wife could not take action against her husband for assault. A case in which a man had beaten his wife with a poker, causing blood to flow from the ears, was tried at Rotherham as late as 1888. Mr Justice Day observed that the prisoner had been merely exercising that control over his wife which was still sanctioned by the law of England. The jury acquitted promptly, as directed.

7. *Appeal*, pp. 105–6.

8. ibid. p. 121.

9. op. cit. p. 148.

10. ibid. p. 170.

11. At the Anti-Slavery Convention of 1840 women delegates who had arrived from America were refused permission to take part, being only allowed to hear the proceedings from behind a curtain. In Northern Germany it was not until the Imperial Law of May 15, 1908, that German women could take part in political organizations and meetings.

12. op. cit. p. 144.

13. op. cit. pp. 157–9.

14. ibid. pp. 199, 204–5, 210–11.

15. op. cit. 188–94, 212.

16. *The Co-operative Magazine and Monthly Herald*, Vol. 1, No. 2, p. 46, 1826.

17. ibid. Vol. I, No. 8, pp. 254–7.

18. Alexander Walker, *Women physiologically examined as to mind, morals, marriage, matrimonial slavery, infidelity and divorce* (1833).

Chapter 10

1. M. Beer, *A History of British Socialism* (1929), Vol. I, p. 187.
2. *The Co-operative Magazine*, Vol. I, No. 1, pp. 22–3; No. 2, pp. 109–10.
3. John George Godard, *George Birkbeck* (1884), p. 98; *Robert Southey, The Story of His Life written by his letters* (edited by John Dennis, 1887), p. 354.

Chapter 11

1. William Thompson, *Labour Rewarded*, pp. 31–8.
2. *Labour Rewarded*, pp. 31–8.
3. ibid. p. 23.
4. *Labour Rewarded*, pp. 39–40, 52–5, 66, 124.
5. *Labour Rewarded*, pp. 22–34.
6. ibid. pp. 32–3.
7. *Labour Rewarded*, p. 36.
8. *Labour Rewarded*, pp. 39–44, 119; *Inquiry*, pp. 270, 594.
9. Arguing the case for the recall of officials, Bentham said that without it, 'the people's right of election would be very inadequate to its end.'
10. *Labour Rewarded*, p. 124.
11. *Labour Rewarded*, pp. 48–50.
12. ibid. pp. 44–5.
13. *Labour Rewarded*, pp. 56–61.
14. *Labour Rewarded*, pp. 69–74, 127.
15. *Labour Rewarded*, pp. 126–7.
16. *Labour Rewarded*, pp. 63, 124–6.

Chapter 12

1. *Inquiry*, p. 249.
2. These arguments, largely ignored in orthodox economic circles at the time, did not make headway in bourgeois circles until John Stuart Mill adopted a similar standpoint a generation later. The view that starvation wages could be raised even within the capitalist system later gave a powerful stimulus on the anti-sweating movements.
3. *Labour Rewarded*, p. 78.
4. ibid. pp. 78 and 84.
5. *Labour Rewarded*, pp. 75–80.
6. *Labour Rewarded*, p. 86, pp. 83–6.

Chapter 13

1. George Jacob Holyoake, *A History of Co-operation* (1908), *passim*; and *The Crisis*, *passim*.
2. *Inquiry*, pp. 151, 163, 281, 318, 326.

3. *Labour Rewarded*, p. 104.
4. ibid. pp. 60, 104; *Inquiry*, pp. 238, 281.
5. *Labour Rewarded*, pp. 294, 566.
6. *Labour Rewarded*, pp. 236–7, 566.

Chapter 14

1. op. cit. p. 525.
2. ibid. pp. 526–32.
3. The law was not remedied in this respect until the Friendly Societies Act of 1846 and the Industrial and Provident Societies Acts of 1852 and 1862.
4. op. cit. pp. 564–6.
5. op. cit. pp. 233, 578.
6. John Stuart Mill took a somewhat similar view remarking 'wherever there is an ascendant class, a large portion of the morality of the country emanates from its class interests, and its feelings of class superiority.'
7. *Inquiry*, pp. 251, 290, 313, 498.
8. *The Co-operative Magazine*, Vol. I, No. 7, pp. 229–32.
9. The question of town and country planning was long to receive the attention of Socialist writers who were perhaps the first to grasp its importance. The *Communist Manifesto* includes the slogan: 'Agriculture and the urban industry to work hand in hand, in such a way as by degrees, to obliterate the distinctions between town and country.'
10. *The Co-operative Magazine*, Vol. I, No. 10, p. 314.
11. News of the Cork Community plans reached France, where Joseph Rey paid homage to the work of William Thompson whom he termed 'one of the most distinguished' of the English Co-operators. See Joseph Rey, *Lettres sur le système de la co-operation mutuelle* (1828), p. 87.

Chapter 15

1. *The Co-operative Magazine*, Vol. III, No. 2, p. 43.
2. *The Co-operative Magazine*, New Series, Nos. 10, 12.
3. op. cit. pp. i-iii.
4. op. cit. pp. 7–9.
5. ibid. pp. 249–50.
6. op. cit. p. 11.
7. *Practical Directions*, p. 45.
8. *Practical Directions*, p. 30.
9. ibid. pp. 83, 145, 151.
10. *Practical Directions*, pp. 27, 30, 105–6.
11. ibid. pp. 29, 181.
12. ibid. pp. 98, 133.
13. *Practical Directions*, pp. 109–12.

14. *Practical Directions*, p. 56.
15. *Practical Directions*, pp. 61–73.
16. ibid. pp. 58, 69.
17. *Practical Directions*, p. iv.
18. ibid. pp. 205, 224–5.

Chapter 16

1. op. cit. p. 389.
2. *Robert Owen Letters*, No. 211.
3. *Resolutions etc passed at the first meeting of the Co-operative Congress*, *passim*.
4. *The Liverpool Chronicle*, June 8, 1831.
5. *The Manchester Guardian*, June 4 and June 11; *The Manchester Times and Gazette*, June 4 and June 11; *Wheeler's Manchester Chronicle*, June 4, 1831; *The Manchester Courier and Lancashire General Advertiser*, June 11, 1831.
6. *Proceedings of the Second Co-operative Congress* (1831), *passim*.
7. The reference is apparently to Marriott's *Catechism on Circumstances*. Thompson declared that 'truth is necessarily progressive,' but that the institutions established to propagate it were 'as necessarily chained down to systems, seldom the best, but the most useful to the governors' in the age when they were established; they were 'always lagging behind succeeding ages.' *Inquiry*, p. 286.
8. *The Life and Struggles of William Lovett* (1876), p. 48.
9. *Proceedings of the Third Co-operative Congress* (1832), *passim*.
10. *The Crisis*, Vol. I, No. 6, p. 23.
11. *Proceedings of the Fourth Co-operative Congress* (1833), pp. 30–1.
12. E. T. Craig, *The Irish Land and Labour Question* (1882), pp. 158–9; William Pare, *Co-operative Agriculture* (1870), pp. 122–3.
13. Thompson's tower was a well-known landmark until the local authorities pulled it down to use the stone for road-making. According to the record still extant kept by a local resident, the tower was a hundred feet high, thirty-five feet in diameter, and had a conical roof. Its foundations may still be discerned nearby at Carrigfodha.

Chapter 17

1. John Minter Morgan, *Hampden in the Nineteenth Century* (1834), Vol. II, pp. 295–8; D. Donovan, *Sketches in Carbery* (1876), *passim*; W. O'Neill Daunt, *A Life Spent in Ireland* (1892), *passim*; E. T. Craig, *The Irish Land and Labour Question* (1882), *passim*.
2. *The Crisis*, Vols. III and IV, *passim*.

Chapter 18

1. The significance of Thompson's writings in regard to the emancipation of women is discussed in Chapters VIII and IX.
2. Harold J. Laski, *Karl Marx* (1922), p. 30.
3. Vide Anton Menger, *Right to the Whole Produce of Labour* (1899), p. xxviii.
4. John Minter Morgan, *Hampden in the Nineteenth Century*, Vol. II, pp. 302–3.
5. Flora Tristan, *Promenades dans Londres* (1840), p. 383; George Jacob Holyoake, *A History of Co-operation* (1908), p. 244.
6. British Museum, Additional MSS. 27,790, pp. 7, 23–4; 27,797, p. 290; 27,819, p. 229.
7. Alexander Bain, *James Mill* (1882), p. 364.
8. Society for the Diffusion of Useful Knowledge, *The Rights of Industry* (1831), *passim*.
9. Mountiford Longfield, *Lectures in Political Economy* (1833), p. 159.
10. Samuel Read, *An Inquiry into the Natural Grounds of Right to Vendible Property or Wealth* (1829), p. xxix.
11. T. Cooper, *Lectures on the Elements of Political Economy* (1826), p. 351.
12. *United Trades' Co-operative Journal*, *passim*.
13. William King, *An Important Address to Trade Unions* (1829).
14. G. D. H. Cole, *A Study in British Trade Union History* in *International Review for Social History*, Vol. IV, p. 409.
15. Friedrich Engels, *The Condition of the Working Class in England in 1844*, p. 237.
16. Harold J. Laski, *Communism* (1927), p. 19.
17. Sidney and Beatrice Webb, *The History of Trade Unionism* (1912), p. 148.
18. The group included Henry Hetherington, Benjamin Warden, William Lovett, Robert Wigg, Philip and George Skene, William Millard, James Watson, John Cleave, George Foskett, Thomas Powell, Julian Hibbert, George Petrie, William Carpenter, James Tucker, Charles Rosser, and Procter.
19. It is interesting to note that the proposal of women's suffrage, for which Thompson and Anna Wheeler had written their *Appeal* a decade earlier, was included by Lovett in the original draft of the 'People's Charter,' though later omitted.

Chapter 19

1. H. L. Beales, *The Early English Socialists* (1933), p. 79.
2. John Stuart Mill, *Autobiography* (1924), p. 297 and *passim*.
3. *Inquiry*, p. 581.
4. John Stuart Mill, *Principles of Political Economy*, p. 200.

Chapter 20

1. Anton Menger, op. cit. pp. 51–6.
2. ibid. pp. 100–1.
3. Karl Marx and Friedrich Engels, *The Communist Manifesto*, introduction by Harold J. Laski, p. 58.
4. Sidney and Beatrice Webb, *The History of Trade Unionism* (edition of 1920), pp. 162–3.
5. H. L. Beales, *The Early English Socialists* (1933), pp. 79, 93.
6. Thomas Hodgskin, *Labour Defended*, introduction by G. D. H. Cole, pp. 15–16.
7. Alfred Marshall, *Principles of Economics* (1890), pp. 619–20.
8. Joseph A. Schumpeter, *Capitalism, Socialism, Democracy* (1943), p. 308.
9. Vladimir Gregorgievitch Simkhovitch, *Marxism versus Socialism* (1923), p. 114 n.
10. Thorstein Veblen, *The Place of Science in Modern Civilization* (1932), pp. 412–13, 491.
11. *Die Neue Zeit* (December 9, 1910), pp. 314–21.
12. Friedrich Engels, op. cit. pp. 230–40.
13. Karl Marx, *The Poverty of Philosophy* (1900), p. iii.
14. ibid. p. iv.
15. ibid. p. 42.
16. *Labour Rewarded*, pp. 7–8.
17. *Practical Directions*, p. 251.
18. *Inquiry*, pp. 164–5.
19. ibid. p. 171.
20. ibid. p. 211.
21. Marx and Engels, *Communist Manifesto* (Ryazanoff edition), p. 39; Marx, *Capital* (1889 translation), Vol. 1, p. 289.
22. *Labour Rewarded*, pp. 40–1.

Index